RESILIENCE

RESILIENCE

Coming Back from Crisis with Faith, Passion and Purpose

ANNIE NELSON

Published by Annie Nelson
Mission Viejo, California

Copyright © 2019 by Annie Nelson. All rights reserved.
Printed in the United States of America.

No part of this book may be reproduced or transmitted in any form or by any means, electronic or mechanical, including photocopying, recording, or by any information storage and retrieval system without written permission of the Author or Publisher, except where permitted by law. Requests for permission should be addressed to Permissions, Annie Nelson, 24000 Alicia Pkwy., Mission Viejo, CA 92691 or online at theannienelson@gmail.com.

Nelson, Annie
    RESILIENCE: Coming Back from Crisis with Faith, Passion and Purpose
    Paperback ISBN: 978-0-578-49844-7
    Ebook ISBN: 978-0-578-49845-4

Limit of Liability/Disclaimer of Warranty: The Publisher and Author make no representations or warranties with respect to the accuracy or completeness of the content of the work and specifically disclaim all warranties, including without limitation warranties of fitness for a particular purpose. No warranty may be created or extended by sales or promotional materials. Neither the Publisher nor the Author shall be liable for loss of profit or any other commercial damages, including but not limited to special, incidental, consequential or other damages.

The purpose of this book is to educate and entertain. The Author or Publisher does not guarantee that anyone following the techniques, suggestions, tips, ideas or strategies will become successful. The Author and Publisher have neither liability or responsibility to anyone with respect to any loss or damage caused, or alleged to be caused, directly or indirectly by the information contained in this book and these writings.

Cover design: Joe Potter
Front and back cover photo credit: Marc Royce Photography
Interior design: Deanne Marie

Praise for RESILIENCE

"Annie is one of those precious and few individuals who in the face of significant personal pain and hardship still finds the time to devote countless hours of their time and energy to support others in need. Her devotion to our wounded warriors is exemplary, and I'm proud to be her supporter and friend."
>– Joe Mantegna
>Tony-Award winning actor and Spokesperson for the National Army Museum

"Annie Nelson's remarkable story of overcoming multiple head trauma, PTSD, and a life-threatening brain tumor, and transforming her adversity into the opportunity to support our veterans and their families, embodies the spirit of my Open Hearts Foundation, for which she won the first-ever 'Open Heart Patriot Award' in 2012. In her memoir, Annie exemplifies how facing life struggles with faith and courage truly can make a difference to others."
>– Jane Seymour
>Award-winning actress, artist, and philanthropist

"Annie Nelson has done about as much as one lovely lady could possibly do to support and truly care about the welfare of our nation's veterans. Her book not only reflects her passion but a true outlook at what all of us should say. God bless these people that put their lives on the line as well as their health so that we may maintain a way of life. May God bless our veterans as much as he blesses our country's future."
>– John Paul DeJoria
>Co-Founder, Paul Mitchell Hair Care
>Co-Founder, Patron Tequila & Spirits

"I've known Annie Nelson for over 35 years and I've never met someone so devoted to causes and helping others as Annie has been all of her life. She puts herself before others and that's one of the many qualities that makes her unique and special. She's faced numerous hardships and obstacles in her life yet that has never stopped her from giving back to others. Her support to the wounded warriors has been so impressive, it's just amazing the time she's given to helping our veterans. Her book is inspiring and can teach others how important it is to persevere and give back."

    – Dara Torres
    5-time Olympian, 12-time Olympic medalist, author, motivational speaker

"Values that are in the heart of every Hall of Famer are perseverance, courage and resilience. Annie Nelson's journey is Hall of Fame worthy and from which we can all find victory even in the face of adversity."

    – David Baker
    President and CEO, Pro Football Hall of Fame

"Annie has spent her life leading by example, turning personal hardship into speeches and writings that have helped countless people get the most out of life. Her decision to focus her energies on our nation's veterans—and the share the full story behind that decision—is a lesson to all of us; we cannot and must not wait for the government to take care of our heroes when they return from war. It is incumbent upon each of us as citizens to shoulder that burden. I couldn't be happier to see people like Annie leading the charge."

    – Chef Robert Irvine
    Star of *Restaurant: Impossible* and founder of The Robert Irvine Foundation

"Annie's life story captured in her book RESILIENCE is reflected in this quote from 2200 years ago: *Aut inveniam viam aut faciam*. We will find a way, or we will make one. (Hannibal, 218 BC) "
    – Scott Brauer
    Founding Partner of Acumen Performance Group and retired Navy SEAL Officer

"Annie Nelson is a SUPER Patriot who has overcome tremendous hurdles in her life, yet continues to give more of herself to others — especially to our military — than just about anyone I know. She is selfless, tireless, and dedicated to serving the men and women who serve us, and keep America safe. We are all lucky to have Annie."
    – Dean Cain
    Actor/Filmmaker

"Annie Nelson has spent her adult life being of service to others in need and a voice for those who lack the appropriate megaphone. Her journey from fear to faith and faith to service is map to fulfillment. We could all learn something from Annie. This book may change you!!"
    – David James Elliott
    Actor, Entrepreneur

"Annie is that rare individual who can courageously manage her own health issues, while skillfully advocating for our nation's heroes, all wrapped up in a vivacious package."
    – Dr. Steven Giannotta
    Chair and Professor of Neurological Surgery, Dr. Martin Weiss Chair in Neurological Surgery, USC Keck University Hospital

"Annie Nelson is a woman whose faith has been tested on many levels. Our Creator has given her the grace and passion to share her experiences with the lives of countless people and especially those who put their lives on the line for all of us. I am grateful for her ability to rebound and affect so many people. I am humbled to be in her circle of friends. People like Annie give me hope and a great resource to share how to bounce back in the most challenging of times."
    – Dave Sanderson
    President, Dave Sanderson Speaks International; author, speaker, mentor

"I've known Annie for years! I've seen her story impact the lives of others and it's been awesome to walk alongside her on her journey. I hope everyone picks up her book *RESILIENCE*, it's a story for all."
    – Jeremiah Workman
    U.S. Marine Corps (Ret.), Recipient of the Navy Cross and Author

"Annie Nelson's book *RESILIENCE* is a must-read for America at this critical time. Too many Americans, especially teenagers, are seeking to find an answer through the cures the culture offers. In the end, they succumb as we see suicide rates skyrocketing in America, certainly for our Veterans. Annie's book reminds us of that rugged American individualism, and spiritual resolve needed to overcome the trials and tribulations of this world ... as it says in John 16:33. Read Annie's book and find your resilience, and inner peace."
    – Lt. Col. Allen B. West (US Army, Ret.)
    Member, 112th US Congress

"Annie is the inspiration that has changed my life along with countless others. Her own struggles have fueled an unwavering passion of personal strength, positive influence, and dedication. Her story shares understanding, connection, support, and the commanding will to fight with love and hope. Never quit."

    – Anthony Ball
    US Army, 1st Sergeant (Ret.)

"My 20-year history treating Annie, she is one of the most resilient, hard working and faith filled people I have treated in my career as a physical therapist. She has an unbelievable positive attitude despite the pain and discomfort she is experiencing daily. This book will encourage and inspire all who read it!"

    – Joe Donohue
    Owner, ProSport Physical Therapy & Performance
    Official Partner of Hoag Orthopedic Institute

"Annie has single-handedly helped more veterans and service members than anyone I have ever worked with. She is a beacon of support in the fog of war. I attribute a lot of my personal successes to her advice and support, truly a sister from another mister."

    – Justin Jordan
    Master Sergeant, U.S. Air Force (Ret.)
    Author, *And Then I Cried: Stories of a Mortuary NCO*

"Annie has been one of the strongest advocates for suicide prevention and awareness in the United States while moving her own personal mountains. If there is a voice you should listen to, Annie is that voice. I have no doubt this book will be great for any person in need of support on a subject matter that is an often difficult, though necessary, discussion."

- Ryan Weaver
Country Music Artist, Former CW3 Blackhawk Aviator (US Army), Gold Star Sibling

"I know what resilience looks like first hand! Annie has beaten the odds and has overcome significant obstacles in life through her positive attitude and her altruistic spirit. Her generosity and love of life is contagious! Even when life seemed limited to her, she fought back and said "not today!" This is the epitome of resilience and Annie is a tremendous example for all of us!"

- Mary Kate Flatley
Leader, coach

"I've known Annie for years, and her passion for giving and supporting everyone, especially veterans, is second to none. There is no one I know who has given more than she has, all while going through struggles and setbacks that would stupefy the average person. She truly defines resilience."

- Joel Lambert
Former Navy SEAL and Host/Producer of survival and adventure shows on Discovery channel and Animal Planet

"Annie's selfless devotion, empathy, and compassion for those around her serves as a shining example of the best of us. She turned her own tragedy into a life's calling and commitment to others, proving to all those around her that life truly is what we make of it."
– David Meadows
Former Navy SEAL, Actor

"To anything in life, you have to be resilient. This book is a must-read for anyone looking to understand the secret for success in any area of life from someone who has more than beat the odds."
– Wayne Elsey
Founder & CEO, Elsey Enterprises, LLC

Dedication

Dedicated to my parents Robert W. and Carol Ann Nelson, the true wind beneath my wings!

In loving memory of my dad RW Nelson
June 12, 1922 – September 7, 2002

Contents

Praise for *RESILIENCE*... i

Dedication.. viii

Acknowledgements xi

Foreword..xiii

1 Back to the beginning..1

2 Flying high, until 15

3 Invisible 31

Pillar #1: Define your situation. 37

4 Back on my feet 43

5 My rock crumbles...47

6 And now this..63

Pillar #2: Make a personal inventory....................................69

7 Finding my mission..73

8 The power of the pen..81

9 An idea takes hold..87

Pillar #3: Create a personal mission statement.....................95

10 We interrupt this program 99

11 The idea takes off.. 105

Pillar #4: Assemble your team.. 111

12 Rewriting the suicide story.. 119

13 The highest high, and another blow 129

Pillar #5: Develop your faith.. 135

Resources 143

Recommended Reading.. 144

About the Author 145

Invite Annie to Speak.. 147

Acknowledgements

I want to take this time to thank those who have all been a big part of my life and my comeback journey, for without these people, resilience would be impossible.

First and foremost, my parents!

Followed by my family especially all the Woltzens—you each know who you are.

Friends including the Harmelink Family, the Cole family, Tracy Pope, Lisa Junker, Lynn Margolis, Frank and Jennifer Wheaton, Marilyn Jorgensen, Tito Ortiz, Nick Searcy and Larry Broughton.

To everyone involved in the American Soldier Network.

To David Baker, Joe Mantegna, Kevin Sorbo, Jane Seymour, Dean Cain, Scott Brauer, Dara Torres, John Paul DeJoria, Wayne Elsey, Dave Sanderson, Chef Robert Irvine, David Meadows, Lt. Col. Allen B. West, David James Elliott, Jeremiah Workman, Anthony Ball, Justin Jordan, Joel Lambert, Ryan Weaver and Mary Kate Flatley not only for your friendships but for also contributing to this book.

My amazing medial team, especially Dr. Steven Giannotta and Dr. Michael Lowenstein.

My physical therapy team Joe Donohue and Laura Scott along with everyone at ProSport Physical Therapy

My churches: Crossline Community Church in Laguna Hills, California; and Impact Church in Scottsdale, Arizona.

Thank you to Jesse Schertz, Adam Schertz and Tyler Ziegel for your service and friendship. Your journeys truly changed the direction of my life and I'm forever grateful.

To ALL our US Military and the Veteran community who have shown me true resilience 24/7!

To my cover photographer Marc Royce.

To Deanne Marie for helping *RESILIENCE* come to life!

Foreword

By Kevin Sorbo
Actor, Producer

In Annie's book, *RESILIENCE: Coming Back from Crisis with Faith, Passion and Purpose*, you will meet the woman I have come to know well, and proudly call "friend." To put it simply, Annie has never met a stranger, nor faced a challenging life event she could not handle. Her infectious smile and engaging personality are genuine, and her compassion for others is sincere.

Annie and I bonded quickly after meeting, upon discovering we shared Minnesota roots and Scandinavian ties. A few years later, Annie and I had yet another reason to connect. In 1997, I had suffered three strokes while filming "Hercules." I kept quiet about my ordeal until 2011, when I authored *True Strength*, which chronicled my ordeal and recovery. Annie likewise faced a devastating medical diagnosis in 2010, when she learned she had a rare brain tumor that would ultimately require more than ten hours of risky, intricate surgery. Annie's positive attitude in confronting her tumor diagnosis, surgery, and treatment was impressive; and I knew well from my own experience how hard she had to fight what could have been a crushing life experience.

But Annie's story does not stop there. After sustaining ongoing personal tragedies and loss, culminating in her brain tumor diagnosis, Annie turned her attention to supporting the military as vigorously as she fought to be healthy. She selflessly has dedicated her time and efforts to support our troops, with a passion that is evident—Annie truly walks the walk in helping the brave men and women who put their lives on the line for our freedom each day.

Annie's story of overcoming tremendous life obstacles with courage, rooted in her deep faith, is an inspirational story vested in "resilience" that will touch your heart. She is a true American hero.

1

Back to the beginning

My dad and I had always been close. I think it's fair to say that I was pretty much his shadow growing up, and according to my mom Carol, I was Dad's everything. He traveled for his work in farm machinery sales at DeLaval every week, coming home on Friday nights until the next week began. Mom and Dad always had "date night" Friday nights, but otherwise he and I were inseparable, and Mom was content to step back and let us have our time, whether we were going to the grocery store together, side-by-side washing his car and my bike, or going to the movies.

At 6'8", I'm not the only one who looked up to Bob Nelson, and for more reasons than one. My father was a kind, gentle giant, known as a "man's man," and a man of his word, caring for his family, his neighbors. He was also a very handsome man, and he had swept my mom off her feet when they met. Mom had been working in a dentist's office and Dad had come in as a patient. Mom was immediately drawn to his warm, beautiful eyes; Dad loved her smile.

Of Norwegian ancestry, Dad was born in 1922, and was 16 years older than my mom when they got married. There was never a formulated plan for my coming into the world — my parents let God make that decision — and I arrived on July 21, 1967, weighing 9 pounds, 8 ½ ounces.

I made my grand entrance on my paternal grandfather's birthday to the delight of everyone in the family, since my grandfather had passed away before my birth. In the 1960s, it was unusual to be a dad for the first time at 45 years old, but my dad relished the idea. Also rare in those days, my dad was a very involved father with my care when I was a baby, though he drew the line at diapers! He carried me everywhere, excited to show off his little girl.

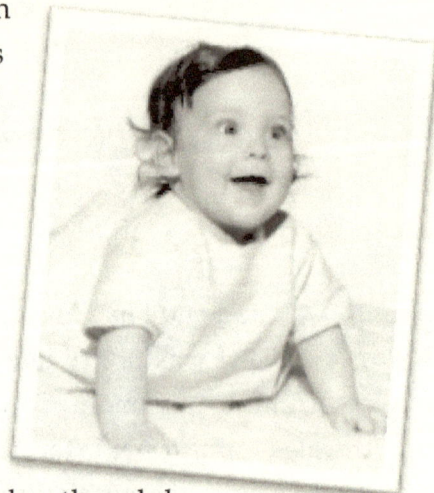

When no other children were forthcoming, my parents decided to adopt to give me a sibling. But when I was three years old, we were transferred from our home in Bloomington, Minnesota, to Palatine, Illinois before they could complete the adoption process. They started the adoption process again after getting settled in the Chicago suburb, and then Dad was transferred a third and final time in 1974, to Mission Viejo, California.

At that point, Dad was 52 years old, and I suppose the thought of having babies and diapers had lost their appeal, but Mom has always said it was okay because he was perfectly happy with what he already had: Me.

From fearful to fearless

The first of the many physical challenges I have faced throughout my life began at birth. Whether due to my size or some other developmental reason, my legs were crooked when I was born. In the 1960s, the remedy was to place my feet in baby shoes that were connected to a steel bar which stretched the width of my shoulders. I slept with my feet in the bar and, as a baby, even crawled dragging the bar behind me, undeterred.

At 16 months, Mom took me for one of my regular orthopedic check-ups. Though the brace was helping, the doctor told my mother that if I learned to ice skate, to use my leg muscles to push off on the ice, I could probably get out of the brace altogether. My mom, born and raised in the Midwest, knew nothing about ice skating, but she was game for anything that would help me.

Since we lived in Minnesota at the time, there was a wonderful new hockey rink just ten minutes from where we lived, the Metropolitan Sports Center in Bloomington. The Met Center, as it was known, was home to a new NHL team franchise, the Minnesota North Stars, and it had also just launched an ice-skating school. After leaving the doctor's office, we traipsed to the rink and Mom spoke to Nanette, one of the instructors. When Mom said that she wanted to enroll me for ice skating classes, Nanette was skeptical. At 16 months, I was far younger than the minimum age that the school required; but upon hearing it was for a medical reason, Nanette relented.

Though Nanette was okay with my taking lessons, there was another problem to overcome: my feet were too small for the ice skates sold in retail shops. Nanette suggested that Mom speak with someone at the famous Oberhamer skate factory in St. Paul to see if they could make me a pair. So, the next day, my mother and I drove 25 miles to St. Paul, where I was fitted for a tiny pair of custom-made ice skates — to the tune of $84 in

1968. That's equivalent to $580 in today's economy! But my parents somehow found the money for my special skates; nothing was too good for their Annie.

The first day of skating class arrived and I wanted nothing to do with being on the ice. I cried. I sat down. I was, in a word, terrified of the slippery, cold ice. The skates felt clumsy on my feet, and I wasn't sure who the ladies on the ice were, but they definitely weren't anybody I knew. I was having none of it, and my mother was disheartened—but certainly not defeated. She insisted that I return to the rink for the next class, and as Mom bundled me in her arms and left the rink, she assured a doubting Nanette that, yes, we *would* be returning.

> *The first day of skating class arrived and I wanted nothing to do with being on the ice.*

The second day of lessons arrived, and I still was resistant to the program. But that particular day, NHL hockey player Bill Collins was sitting in the stands, waiting for practice to start. As he watched the scene at the edge of the rink unfold with some amusement (and a lot of understanding) at both my reluctance and my mother's predicament, he made a decision that changed my life. Wanting to be helpful, he approached my mom and asked if he could take me out on the ice. Knowing that I was comfortable with men since I had bonded so closely with my dad, she gratefully said yes.

Bill reached for my small, outstretched hand and gently led me out onto the ice, where he helped me balance on my skates, zooming me carefully along the rink's slick surface, making a game of gliding along the cold, wet ice. My mother held her breath, tears filling her eyes, as she began laughing in chorus with my giggling, which echoed loudly in the near-empty rink. I loved it, my blond hair flying as Bill whisked me the full length of the rink and back again, over and over, until he finally returned me to my mother's welcome arms.

After that, I eagerly looked forward to my ice skating lessons, and, with the same determination to achieve that has held me in good stead in other circumstances through the years, I learned quickly. The use of the muscles required in skating did, indeed, produce the desired medical effect on my leg strength, and the leg brace became no longer necessary. Soon, I was skating fearlessly, attempting leaps and turns as I worked hard to keep up with the older kids in class, happily racing onto the ice at every opportunity.

Better still, confidently clutching a small, custom-made ice hockey stick, I led the Minnesota North Stars out onto the ice at every home game, including the seventh game of the Western Division playoffs for the Stanley Cup against the St. Louis Blues that ended in a loss after double-overtime. I, of course, never saw the ending of the game—but the beginning of the game? That was all mine.

A chance meeting

My childhood was fairly typical for an upper-middle class family in the U.S. during the '60s, '70s, and early '80s. We had a sprawling split-level home with a pool in Mission Viejo, where I attended elementary, junior high, and high school. I joined the Blue Birds, took piano and violin lessons, and was active in drama club and marching band. There were dance lessons and swimming lessons, team sports and individual sports, though I had stopped ice skating when we moved to California.

My parents were very involved with my school and after-school activities, always volunteering to have the meetings or parties at our house. My friends and teammates even called my parents, "Mom and Dad Nelson," because they were always offering to help in any way they could.

We often went on family excursions in our Southern California community. The summer of 1976, my parents took me to see an Oakland A's game at the stadium in Anaheim. At nine years old, I was as excited about the hot dogs, popcorn, and Oakland A's pennant my parents bought me, as I was the game. The sights and sounds inside the stadium were noisy and fun. It was a beautiful, sunny day under a typical Southern California sky. My parents were having a great time, too, enjoying a relaxing afternoon at the ballpark. After the game was over, I noticed a bunch of kids going down toward the field to get autographs of the players. I turned to my parents and said,

"I want to go down there and meet the players! Pleeeeeeaseee?" with the biggest smile I could muster — you know, the one your parents rarely say "no" to.

My dad nodded and smiled as Mom took me by the hand and led me down toward the field, fishing a piece of paper and a pencil out of her purse along the way. She stopped on the bottom step of the stadium as I ran onto the field, paper and pencil in hand, and over to the A's catcher, Jeff Newman.

"Mr. New-Man, may I have your name?"

Newman laughed, and replied, "Sure, but you don't want to have an old piece of paper for an autograph. Hold on."

With that, he went over to the dugout and got a baseball and signed it, then corralled his teammates to do the same.

"Where are your folks, Annie?" Jeff asked, handing me the autographed baseball, my eyes wide with surprise as the other kids started looking my way.

"That's my mom over there," I said excitedly, pointing to her down in front, "and that's my dad up there!"

Seeing me gesturing, my dad waved, and my mother walked over to where we were standing.

"Nice to meet you, Annie's mom," Newman said. "This is my new girlfriend, and we're all going to go out for ice cream, my treat, so meet me at Gate One in about 15 minutes." With that, he smiled and sprinted toward the showers.

I was so excited! We climbed the concrete stadium half-steps to my dad, and Mom relayed what Newman had said as I bounced up and down at the prospect of ice cream with the A's catcher.

"Carol, there's no way he's going to do that," Dad said, shaking his head, chuckling at Mom's naivete.

"No, really, Bob! He seemed genuine, he really appeared to mean it! I think we should get over to Gate One!" Mom insisted.

We no sooner made our way to Gate One, than Jeff Newman came running up. He introduced himself to my dad, took me by the hand, and we all headed to our car.

"I don't know where there's ice cream around here," he said, "but our hotel is near Disneyland, I'm sure we can find something near there."

Soon, we were all sitting at a local Baskin Robbins, talking, laughing, and eating our ice cream on the warm summer's day. After a few hours, we said our good-byes, and as Jeff headed toward his hotel he turned and said,

"See you at the game tomorrow night!"

My parents hesitated, and finally Dad said a little awkwardly, "Well, uh, we won't be back for tomorrow's game, this was a special occasion, we only had tickets for today."

"No worries, Mr. Nelson," Jeff replied, "when we're in town, you're always my guests. You're my baseball family now."

For the next six seasons while Jeff played for the Oakland A's, we went to all the games as Jeff's guests when the team played in Anaheim. We met Jeff's wife, and even traveled to Oakland on numerous occasions to see Jeff play. He introduced us to the other Oakland A's players, and we got to know many of them, too.

In 1982, Jeff was traded to the Boston Red Sox, and some of the A's ballplayers we knew were traded to other teams, too. When the Red Sox played in California, we were his guests at the games in California yet again. Then, other team members who had been traded to the Yankees, the Orioles, and other teams, would call the house before a game in California: "Hey Mom Nelson" or "Hey Dad Nelson, are you guys coming to the game?" and we always went. Our "family-by-heart" team members have stayed close to this day; Mom and I even flew to the Baseball Hall of Fame when Jim Rice and Ricky Henderson were inducted.

It's amazing to think that a chance encounter—if you believe in such things—when I was nine years old seeking an autograph at a baseball game in Anaheim would lead to a lifetime of friendships among major league baseball teams across the country.

But such events have continued to happen in my life, for whatever reason I do not know.

Somehow, the opportunities to be a part of many kinds of "teams" multiplied from that one beautiful summer's day back in 1976, when Jeff Newman first took my family for ice cream.

Hollywood was calling

Like many children, I had acting aspirations growing up, so I started attending the Laguna Moulton Theatre in 1976. I was in the fourth grade, and my acting coach was Lisa Surette. Not only was Southern California the perfect place to explore my budding acting interest, but Mom had known McLean "Uncle Mac" Stevenson from her childhood days in Illinois.

One day while we were visiting Uncle Mac, I told him that even though I was in theatre classes, what I *really* wanted was to be on television and in the movies. Uncle Mac arranged for me to be Farrah Fawcett's "ball girl" on "Battle of the Network Stars."

To this day, I don't know how he did it, but we got the call asking me to participate. Mom was all for it, but Dad was not. Though my dad was reluctant, he finally relented, and I loved it! Not only did I get to run around as Farrah's ball girl, I got to hang out with her and Lee Majors, too. Pretty cool!

Here I was, a little girl from Minnesota, hanging out with Farrah Fawcett and Lee Majors! It was heaven for me. I think that's also when I first realized other people felt the camera and I were friends.

I reached my full height of 5'10" when I turned 13. Being tall finally had advantages! Every Saturday, Mom and Dad would drive me to Los Angeles to meet with my modeling coach, Beryl Barone. She was tough! I trained to be a ramp (runway) model, and soon I was signed on with modeling Mary Webb Davis.

> *Here I was, a little girl from Minnesota, hanging out with Farrah Fawcett and Lee Majors!*

I also started auditioning for television and film, and appeared on "C.H.I.P.S." as part of the "Brat Patrol" episodes. The work on set was fun, and the playtime off set was, too, when Erik Estrada, Bruce Penhall, and other cast members would hang around with us kids, as we rode around the MGM lot on our bikes. Even though it was a non-scripted role, being on set was the best feeling ever. I was hooked.

A big acting opportunity came up when I read for a regular role on a new television series. I got a callback for the part with the director, but my dad summarily put his foot down; I could seriously pursue acting after I was 18, but not before. He was afraid of the business for his little girl, and though it hurt at the time, I know it was motivated by loving me.

Undeterred, I did pursue my acting after I graduated from high school, attending California State University in Long Beach on a theatre arts scholarship.

But my attention was not on theatre, so I quickly abandoned that major, and found myself drawn to broadcast journalism. I was able to work while in school at KABC – the ABC affiliate in Los Angeles – with legendary sports broadcaster Ted Dawson. Some of the stories I prepared for class were actually aired on KABC, yet I kept receiving only average grades for those on-air pieces. I was learning more from working with Ted than my professors at that point and, disillusioned, I withdrew from the journalism program.

Now a junior in college, I found myself floundering for the first time in my life. I had always been goal-driven, and here I was, 20 years old, without a goal. I knew I loved being in front of the camera, and I knew I wanted to make a difference. At the time, I didn't know how to put those two things together.

Then, out of the blue, I was contacted by Professor Buck of the communications department, which was separate in those days from the journalism school. Dr. Buck brought along Dr. Craig Smith, who later founded the Center for First Amendment Studies. Dr. Smith had served as a full-time speechwriter to President Ford and Lee Iacocca at that time.

I found myself floundering for the first time in my life.

The two professors invited me to lunch to talk about my college career. I was intrigued, honored, and curious, and I listened attentively as they outlined why they felt I should change my major to communications, including putting me on the speech team. I leapt at the opportunity, especially when they told me that they would craft my major so that I would receive credit for all of the outside broadcast journalism work I was still doing with Ted Dawson. I have no idea how they knew I was without a major (divine intervention?) but it was a no-brainer, and my academic career was back on track.

My time working with Ted included his covering the Dallas Cowboys during their training camp time in nearby Thousand Oaks. Those three-plus years from late 1985 through 1989 laid important foundational groundwork for the on-camera work that would follow in later years of my professional career. My reel from that time (which was recorded on an 8-track tape!) included interviews with Herschel Walker, Troy Aikman, Jeff Rohrer, and Jimmy Johnson.

I was tremendously blessed to have had the opportunity to actively participate in my chosen field of study, and I graduated in four years with a Bachelors of Arts Degree in Communications.

After graduation, though I had a degree in communications and had compiled significant on-air time in the broadcast journalism field for someone my age, my heart still pulled me toward acting and the world of entertainment.

I briefly studied at the American Film Institute under Lou Diamond Phillips, and Lou was terrifically supportive of my continuing the pursuit of an acting career. In 1990, I was cast in a film his then-wife Julie was making, "Demon Wind," as one of the demons! It was a fun shoot, complete with extensive demon make-up. I learned a lot about filmmaking and doing stunts from being on set, which was helpful, though the role itself was not particularly memorable.

During that same period of time, I also was hired to appear as the lead in an industrial film for the State of California, "Drug Baby," playing a foster mom who took care of a drug mom's child. It seemed my acting career was slowly starting, but then the opportunities stalled out. Disheartened, I spoke with my agent and asked for honest feedback. If there were anything else I needed to do, anything I could do better, I wanted to know. I was determined. I was committed. I was willing to do whatever it took. Bring it on. I would create and work toward the goal.

The response was not what I wanted to hear: I was too tall. In the early 1990s, height was not the asset it is seen as today. In the days before extensive cable and digital media platforms, there were less opportunities for actors who were not in the center of the bell curve physically. In those days, "bell curve" meant being 5'6" and a size 2, which I surely was not. And while there might be some opportunities, the road ahead as a full-time actress was simply limited by my height.

Despite a mix of emotions, I made the conscious decision to step away from my love of acting; and that's when my career *really* took off — but not how you think.

2

Flying high, until ...

Lisa Cole has been one of my best friends for decades. We actually met at a mutual family friend's wedding when I was ten and Lisa was an "older girl," a very cool 12 years old. Our dads knew one another, and since she was from North Dakota and I was from Minnesota, we bonded rather quickly.

Lisa and I stayed in touch through actual letters as kids after that. As an adult, Lisa married and had three children; she worked as a flight attendant for Southwest Airlines. Lisa was having a blast flying around the country, and the Southwest pay scale was better than any other airline at the time.

Out of school, having stepped away from pursuing a career as an actress, and in need of a "real job," I believed that working as a flight attendant would give me the greatest financial stability coupled with the greatest flexibility, so that I could pursue work in broadcasting, focusing on hosting and on-air magazine-style platforms, where my height didn't matter. I also thought it would be a nice perk for my parents to be able to travel on the family pass that flight attendants received.

The competition for flight attendant positions on Southwest was fierce. I applied at the beginning of 1994 at the age of 25, and was fortunate to be hired quickly. The final hurdle to beginning flight attendant training school was a physical. The examination had revealed a genetic problem that everyone else had missed my entire life: I had patella subluxation on both knees. My kneecaps, to put it plainly, were in the wrong place.

When I heard the news, I had conflicting feelings. First, I was frustrated that I hadn't passed the physical, and I was anxious to find out how this would — or would not — impact my hiring status with Southwest.

But to be honest, a part of me felt relieved and somewhat vindicated, too. My whole life, running had hurt me badly. I hated P.E. class growing up because it was so painful to run. Other than my brief stint playing Bobby Sox softball, I avoided sports activities where running was required, the pain was so great. No one ever knew why, and many teachers and coaches alluded to my not wanting to run being for another reason. I finally had an answer, and it was a genetic one.

More importantly, this was something that could be fixed. Fortunately, Southwest promised to allow me to work if I had the necessary corrective surgery. I immediately had both knees operated on in one day, and within a short time was able to report for flight attendant training school. I was on my way!

I was based out of several airports during my first year at Southwest: Dallas Love Field, Chicago Midway, Phoenix, and then I was fortunate to be a part of the new base that opened in Oakland. I enjoyed the flight attendant work immensely, whether helping the customers, or sometimes making them laugh with fun, humorous announcements.

My parents had always raised me on the adage, "If you can't do it right, don't do it at all," and I had lived by that philosophy my whole life. Still do. So, not surprisingly, I did everything in my power each day on the job to provide

exemplary service. I relished being a team player at the employee-friendly workplace; I was proud of "my" airline.

Within the first few months of flying for Southwest, the airline received its first unsolicited letter of praise from a

Southwest passenger about my job performance. It felt good to receive a memo from "Herb and Colleen" (Chairman of the Board Herbert Kelleher and President Emerita Colleen Barrett), congratulating me on a job well-done.

The day my life changed

December 30, 1994 began like most days on the job. I was flying the last day of a four-day trip flying from Albuquerque, New Mexico, to Los Angeles; and then from Los Angeles to Oakland. We were a five-person crew that day on a Boeing 737-200 aircraft, which has a center aisle, and a 3-and-3 seat configuration.

Captain John Mahoney and First Officer Bob Thomas were based out of Phoenix; and flight attendants Frank Flanders, D'Bora Terrant, and I were based out of Oakland. The flight was Frank's first flight out of training school, and he was assigned to the middle of the plane. D'Bora was senior; she was in the back of the plane. I was assigned to the front.

The trip so far had been exhausting, more than most. Holiday crowds transporting gifts coupled with an impending New Year's Eve party mentality contributed to a higher-than-normal level of chaos. In addition, a huge snowstorm was barreling its way toward Albuquerque, and we had been advised that our flight was going to be the last flight out before the airport was closed. The maintenance crew was busy de-icing the plane, and the ground crew was trying to get the passengers' lined up in numerical order so we could board everyone quickly. Even though the flight was midday, the skies were quickly darkening as the storm approached; we needed to get underway, fast.

*The trip so far had been exhausting,
more than most.*

Captain Mahoney and I were standing on the jetway just before the passengers were released in the jetway to board. Suddenly, a small, young, blond woman came running down toward us. To this day, I don't know how she managed to get down the jetway to where we were standing. She had on a pair of black jeans and a white frilly top, and she looked scattered and a bit disheveled.

"Have you seen my baby?" she asked, surprisingly calm. The Captain and I both responded we had not, and the woman continued, throwing her hands up in the air,

"Uh!! Lost my baby, again!" and with that she ran back up the jetway.

Capt. Mahoney and I stood there incredulously for a moment. What she said was mildly alarming; but the casual manner in which she said it was even more disturbing. We both shook our heads, and refocused on the task at hand—getting airborne. I was particularly stressed about not being stuck in Albuquerque because my childhood best friend, Jackie Meyers, was getting married in Huntington Beach, California, the next day, and I was in the wedding.

As I stood at the entrance to the plane, I could see passengers approaching. The small blonde woman was first, with the errant 2-year old little girl wiggling in her arms. She immediately went to the front of the plane where there was lounge seating, and proceeded to block the aisle for the other boarding passengers as she was settling in with her diaper bag and carry-on luggage. The progress of the line stopped, and a low grumbling among the other waiting passengers began.

I walked over to where the woman stood, still blocking the aisle, and politely asked her to allow others to get by. Instead of responding (apologetically or otherwise) to my reasonable request, the woman proceeded to put her baby on the floor of the aisle and change the nastiest, smelliest, foulest dirty diaper I had ever—or to this day, have ever—witnessed. She had absolutely no awareness of anyone else around her trying to get past, nor how offensive her diaper-changing antics were to the other passengers just walking onto the plane. To say that the diaper was "malodorous" would be a gross understatement. It was just plain awful.

After removing the dirty diaper, she tried to hand it to me. "Here, take this," she said brusquely, extending the dirty diaper.

Due to FAA regulations about how to handle bodily fluids, I could not legally take the diaper in hand without plastic gloves on. I was not about to be fined because of this woman's rudeness, but ever the smiling flight attendant, I asked her to wait a moment. I retrieved a plastic bag, which I held open for her to place the dirty diaper.

The woman was furious that I hadn't immediately taken her baby's filthy diaper in my bare hands. It was all about her. She had absolutely no understanding or awareness that I had more to do to help the captain push back from the gate in advance of a blizzard, than to stop everything for her. As I held the plastic bag open for her, she purposely slammed the diaper into it, nearly ripping the bag from my hands. I still smiled, tightly closed the bag, disposed of it appropriately, and quickly returned to my required pre-flight tasks.

In the meantime, her daughter had disappeared, and the woman was, yet again, searching for the active child. We needn't have worried. Less than a minute later, Captain Mahoney called me to the cockpit, where the little girl was sitting on the floor, laughing. I asked the woman to please retrieve her child, and she laughingly grabbed the baby while flirtatiously giggling and batting her eyes at the pilot. He was not amused, or even mildly interested. The woman flounced back to her seat.

After getting the woman, her child, and all of the other passengers strapped in, we were finally ready to push back from the gate. Captain Mahoney did a great job of hurriedly moving the plane toward the runway, and I felt relieved for the first time in the last hour. Unfortunately, my state of relaxation didn't last long.

As we were taxiing to get in position to take-off, I picked up the microphone and proceeded to give the standard seatbelt, oxygen, and evacuation directions to the passengers, as Frank and D'Bora demonstrated.

While Frank was illustrating how to fasten the seatbelt, the blond woman (yes, her again) tugged at Frank's shirt, and said haughtily and loudly enough for all of the passengers in the front of the plane to hear, "Don't you think you need to show me how to do that, since *she* wants to run the rest of my life?" nodding in my direction. (I have no idea what she was talking about!)

At this point, to be honest, I'd just about had it with this woman, as had all of the other passengers around her. I smiled and slowly, deliberately, said into the microphone, with as much restraint as I could muster under the circumstances,

"Ladies and gentlemen, we have a *very* special guest up front who needs her own personal seatbelt demonstration, we'll be back with *you* in *just* one minute."

With that, I went to the cockpit and asked the Captain to have the woman removed at our first stop in Los Angeles instead of her final destination of Oakland, as it was abundantly clear that she was going to continue to cause problems for the other passengers.

I was also concerned that during the flight there might be some safety issues, given her flagrant disregard of my authority, an intuitive glimpse that unfortunately would hold true.

When I explained what had been happening, the captain offered to return to the gate since we were still on the ground. But mindful of the time pressure, the storm, and the inconvenience of the passengers, I declined. Captain Mahoney concurred with my assessment that the woman and her child should be removed from the flight, and as we continued to taxi, he called ahead to Los Angeles to make the arrangements.

It wasn't often that a customer got under my skin. Actually, I can't remember anyone else whose rudeness, sarcasm, inconsideration, and flat-out disrespect rose to the level of this passenger's. To be honest, as I exited the cockpit, a part of me was secretly happy that she was going to be held accountable for her outlandish behavior when we got to Los Angeles. It was unfair to the other people on the plane, and it was likewise unfair to the crew, that she thought the rules during boarding and flight weren't meant for her.

Captain Mahoney concurred with my assessment that the woman and her child should be removed from the flight.

"Just wait until we get to Los Angeles," I thought, trying to hide a smile. Like a Mama Bear, I was going to make sure that my job keeping the other passengers safe was done to the utmost of my ability, and that this woman would not be rewarded for her unacceptable behavior. It simply wasn't right.

Shortly after we completed the necessary on-ground checks and I had let D'Bora know about the situation, the Captain had the crew take our seats for takeoff. I was seated in the jump seats near the front door. From my seat, I could see the front lounge area on the right side of the plane. The woman was in my line of sight.

FAA regulations require that a plane be at least 10,000 feet before the flight crew can move about the cabin. Our plane had no sooner lifted wheels off the ground, when loud shouting started in the front of the plane.

I'm sure it is no surprise that the woman—seated on the aisle, facing backwards in the lounge configuration of seats that Southwest favored in those days—was arguing with a man seated across from her diagonally in the window seat. The guy had a cast on his arm and was waving it around as he and she were shouting.

Because the 737-200 is somewhat noisy, I couldn't make out exactly what was being said, but sporadic curse words rose above the din—curse words most often associated with people living in New York City, if you know what I mean. I unbuckled my seat belt and approached them.

"Folks, could you please curtail your bickering? You're disturbing other passengers," I asked with as much professional courtesy I could muster.

I might as well have been Casper the Ghost himself. Both the woman and the man with the cast totally ignored me and continued their screaming cussing match as the plane was climbing. The other passengers were looking away, looking anywhere but at the two causing the disturbance.

They finally settled down (or so I thought) and I walked to the back of the plane to inform D'Bora that we needed to not serve alcohol on the flight. I could only imagine how the introduction of alcohol would inflame the volatile situation. D'Bora agreed. That said, D'Bora and I decided to quickly serve the snacks, figuring that if one or both of the two causing the problem were drunk, perhaps eating something would help. We hastily put the snack baskets together, and D'Bora indicated she would advise the Captain and First Officer of the updated situation once we reached 10,000 feet.

I hurriedly walked toward the front of the plane and handed Frank his snack basket, cluing him in as to what D'Bora and I had discussed. Frank was in the center of the cabin and began handing out his snacks. I returned to my section in the front, facing the back of the plane and working my way forward. Suddenly, all of the call buttons started going off behind me, like a chorus of incessant chimes on a windy day.

As I turned around, looking in the direction of the problem duo, I saw that another man was on top of the woman, choking her. The woman was trying to scream and was attempting to kick the man between his legs, her child wedged underneath the man, when suddenly the man with the cast leapt up and lunged into the melee.

I threw my snack basket at Frank—I'm not really sure where it landed—and grabbed the man who was doing the choking in one hand, while trying to push the man with the cast away with my other. The little girl had crawled—or fallen?—onto the floor between my feet. As I was stretched to the max trying to separate the two men, the woman somehow got away and ran into the bathroom, notably leaving her child behind on the floor. The men didn't even seem to notice she was gone, they started going after one another, swinging wildly. But instead of hitting one another, I took a bad hit in the back and was forcibly thrown headfirst into the wall that separates the seating area from the galley.

The wind was completely knocked out of me. I couldn't breathe, but I somehow managed to make my way into the cockpit. I still couldn't breathe when I entered, and though I tried to talk, nothing came out. I was pointing at my back, trying to say, "hit." I collapsed onto the console and somehow mistakenly hit the radio button for all of the Southwest planes in the air, broadcasting our problem live throughout the entire Southwest fleet. The only words I managed to squeak out that Captain Mahoney and First Officer Thomas understood were "hit" and "fight."

> *I couldn't breathe, but I somehow managed to make my way into the cockpit.*

While I was in the cockpit, the fighting between the two men was continuing, and Frank was attempting to separate them. When First Officer Thomas and I returned to the out-of-control passengers, they realized that they were in serious trouble, and immediately calmed down.

At that very moment, the woman who had started the whole problem blasted through the bathroom door and shoved her way past First Officer Thomas and me, and then impatiently attempted to get past Frank, clearly headed to her former seat. Unbelievably, the woman still had no concept of the impact of her actions on those around her.

Frank was standing next to the two unruly men near her seat, as the woman plowed past us, continuing, almost knocking down First Officer Thomas. He instinctively and quickly grabbed her by the wrists, and the passengers started chanting, "Strap her down! Strap her down!" Staying strictly professional, First Officer Thomas firmly sat the woman in her seat and retrieved her child, who had wandered to the galley.

He then removed the man who had been choking the woman and placed him in a seat near the emergency exit of the plane, where he stayed for the duration of the flight. The man with the cast and the woman were subdued, sitting in their respective seats sullenly and quietly without further incident.

At the same time First Officer Thomas and Frank were securing the cabin, Captain Mahoney was contacting Phoenix Airport. He requested an emergency landing, which was granted. When the Captain made the announcement that the plane was diverting to Phoenix, a slight audible groan arose from some of the passengers, but for the most part everyone remained quiet and calm. I made my way to the cockpit and sat in the jumpseat for landing.

My hands began shaking uncontrollably as adrenaline coursed through my body, but otherwise I was totally numb. The whole situation was surreal. No amount of training had prepared me for what I had just witnessed and experienced. I couldn't stop shaking. The awareness of my personal vulnerability in that circumstance kept rising in my consciousness, and I summarily pushed it back down. Avoidance was a useful weapon at that moment, and I was fully locked and loaded.

We had been in the air for slightly less than an hour before hitting the ground again. Because the pilot had declared an emergency landing, it looked like the cavalry was chasing the plane. We were met with firetrucks and police on the runway that escorted us to the gate.

After taxiing to the designated gate, the jetway secure, Frank opened the airplane door. Police officers, firefighters, and Southwest ground personnel had all been waiting for us to arrive. The waiting personnel swarmed onto the plane as the captain stepped out of the cockpit. He pointed to the woman and both men, and said, "I want these three people arrested, and that child needs to be placed in protective child custody," he said.

Avoidance was a useful weapon at that moment, and I was fully locked and loaded.

When the law enforcement officers headed toward the woman, she began screaming, "Don't take my baby! Don't take my baby!" and was escorted off the plane in handcuffs with her child in tow, as were the two men involved in the fight. The passengers cheered after the three were removed, and all of the crew were relieved that a worse situation had been averted. As far as we knew at that point, the woman and two men were arrested and justice was served.

Captain Mahoney then turned to someone from Southwest's Phoenix ground staff and asked that I be replaced on the flight. He was told there was no one to take my place, and I would have to continue to LA. My knees went a little weak hearing that. Looking back, I was probably in shock. I tried to smile at Captain Mahoney, but he was furious. It was insane that I be made to fly after what had happened.

As odd as this may sound, the need to outwardly appear as if everything were fine was the one strand of strength that kept me going at that moment. If I focused on the well-being of the passengers and displayed a "brave soldier" attitude, I reasoned, I would actually *be* okay. Also, a crew change would have meant that the passengers would have a longer wait. I held onto that thought to summon the strength and courage to make it to LA. We secured the cabin in preparation for the next leg of the flight and quickly took off once again.

The 90-minute flight from Phoenix to Los Angeles was fairly uneventful insofar as the passengers were concerned, but I started feeling horrible physically. And for obvious reasons, I was still very upset. All I could think of was getting to LA and going home to Mission Viejo. Captain Mahoney called ahead, insisting that I be replaced at LAX, but he was told it wasn't possible, there were no flight attendants available to take over for me because none had had enough mandatory ground time. I ended up having to complete the flight through to Oakland.

Unbelievably, because I was a "commuter" flight attendant out of Los Angeles, it was my responsibility to either hop a flight back to LAX that night (and there were none because it was so late), or, literally adding insult to injury, pay for my own hotel that night in Oakland.

In a gesture of absolute compassion and thoughtfulness, Captain Mahoney and First Officer Thomas took D'Bora and me to their hotel and paid for a room for us. They kept me awake through the night to make sure I didn't have a concussion, and in the morning, I flew home and actually made the wedding, albeit barely on time. There was no way I was going to miss my best friend's wedding when I had already missed the rehearsal, rehearsal dinner, and all the pre-wedding festivities!

I then went home and straight to bed.

3

Invisible

Over the course of the next few months, my life was dominated by medical issues. I had surgery in mid-January on my knees as a follow-up to my pre-employment surgery, which had been planned long before the events of December 30. I was out of work for nine weeks because of the knee surgery, and during that time I also had time to rest from the trauma of the on-flight brawl. I thought that the rest would help my back pain and headaches. It didn't.

The weekend after the assault I had flown up to Oakland to see a worker's compensation doctor. He barely examined me before sending me to physical therapy. At least I could go to a therapist close to my home in Orange County.

During the initial spinal examination at the physical therapy appointment, I practically flew off the table from pain when the physical therapist gently touched a spot on my lower back. She immediately stopped the exam and insisted I have my back x-rayed.

Later that day, I sat quietly in the work comp doctor's office as he informed me I had an anterior wedge-type flexion compression fracture of approximately 20 to 25 percent at the T12 vertebra. In other words, I had sustained a fracture in my spinal cord as a result of being struck during the fight on the airplane.

In disbelief, I listened as the doctor explained that over time the fracture would close on its own. In the meantime, I would need to rest, have physical therapy, and respond to the pain with medication as needed. During the course of the next year and a half, life was a blur of doctor's visits, CT scans, MRIs, pain medication, trigger point injections, and physical therapy.

Pain dominated my life. I tried to work, but there were times I simply couldn't. I went from being a flight attendant held in high regard, receiving unsolicited praise from passengers and fellow crew members, to struggling to even do my job.

But my physical ability to work as a flight attendant was not the only part of my life that was affected. My emotional life was scarred as well. I had nightmares of the fight. When I was in crowded situations, whether as passengers boarded on the plane or when I was in public, such as the mall or at a restaurant, I was anxious and nervous if anyone came up behind me. Flashbacks of the fight replayed in my mind unwillingly.

> *Pain dominated my life. I tried to work, but there were times I simply couldn't.*

Every day was gauged by how I felt physically; what level of pain I was experiencing (I was never pain free again). I was tired all of the time. I was doing everything I knew to do to get better, but nothing worked.

Invisible wounds

On top of it all, since the injury to my back was not obvious or visible — I wasn't in a cast or on crutches, for example — people did not understand what I was going through mentally, emotionally, or physically. I felt defensive about my physical state. I was angry this had happened to me, when I was only doing my job—a job I had always taken such pride in doing. This wasn't me. I was not the kind of person to complain. At 29 years old, with my whole life before me, I just wanted my life back.

To add insult to injury, I learned that after the disruptive passengers were escorted off the plane and our plane had departed, Southwest ground personnel had met the police inside the terminal and had refused to press charges. The three passengers were immediately released from police custody. One lived in Phoenix and returned home while the other two were put up at the Radisson overnight and placed on another Southwest flight to each of their respective destinations the next day. My health—my life—was in shambles, while the passengers went along their merry way.

It was as if nothing of any significance had really happened at 30,000 feet. I felt invisible.

It is hard to imagine such events unfolding today in a post-9/11 world, but beforehand, the customer was always right, even when there was a physical assault, as happened with me.

Ultimately, I realized that although I couldn't control the events that had unfolded when I was injured, I could surely control my response. After trying to stick it out in my position as a flight attendant for slightly more than a year after the onboard fight, I finally had to accept I could not do my job. I left Southwest Airlines in 1996.

I then resolved to be the healthiest I could be; to learn to live with whatever limitations I might have; and to get on with my life, instead of railing against the injustice of what I was no longer capable of doing. There simply was no other choice.

My back may have been broken on December 30, 1994; but my spirit was decidedly not.

Facing the challenge

During the next year, my life continued to be dominated by multiple physical therapy appointments and doctor appointments each week to assess and assuage the ongoing pain in my back, neck and head. I had started experiencing weakness in my arms, as well, due to nerve damage and issues with Thoracic Outlet Syndrome. Essentially, the nerves between my collarbone and first rib were being compressed due to a previous car accident.

To put it mildly, in 1997, my goal was to get through each day as unscathed as possible. One day at a time? Sometimes it was one hour at a time; and sometimes, even the minutes themselves were unbearable moments.

The long days of recovery stretched from 1997 to 1998, then another year, and another. I tried to keep on a "happy face," but it took a lot of effort to pretend that I was okay when I wasn't, even if I looked as if nothing were wrong with me. That was hard, too. When your pain and injuries aren't visible to the naked eye, after a while there is a presumption of malingering, or even a predilection for the pain medication. I suffered both silent accusations from many, and it hurt. Deeply. Anyone who professed to really know me should have known that I wasn't capable of either. It was yet another "hit" whose impact was hurtful in more ways than one.

I withdrew from activities that weren't absolutely essential. I didn't have the strength to explain the many implications of that fateful day on the airplane, and didn't want to relive it in the telling of the story (the flashbacks were bad enough on their own), so I communicated less and less with people in my life, other than those who really mattered — and I distanced myself from even some of those people.

I wondered what God's plan was for me, that I would have my life turned so upside down at a time when I should have been taking on the world. I was in my early 30s! This was the prime time of my life! *This* Annie was not me. This was *not* what I wanted for my life. Most of the time, I didn't feel like I was getting better, the domino effect seemed to be in play, with one injury causing another symptom, and another, my body in complete rebellion and utter chaos.

In the darkness of the night, I wondered: Would it always be like this? Is this the best I will ever feel? Is *this* going to be my life? There was no pity to those questions, only fear. I had started on a course of recovery with the belief my efforts would take me back to my "normal" self; the realization that this might be my "new normal" scared me to death.

> *In the darkness of the night, I wondered:*
> *Would it always be like this?*

At times, I felt as if my body were betraying me. It simply would not respond to my inner commands. My vision remained blurred during a bad headache, even though I wanted to see clearly. My arms still were tingling and numb, despite my wanting the feeling to stop. Some days, I could not summon the strength to get out of bed except for the necessary trek to the bathroom, a feat which seemed almost insurmountable each time. And yet, no amount of prayer or willpower could override the very real physical challenges I was experiencing.

Did I ask why? Why me? Sure, I did. But each time such doubts raised their ugliness, I turned to my faith and trusted that my needs would be met; that God would get me through this. I knew that there had to be some greater purpose to all that I was going through. And one day, the realization slowly clicked in: The pain, the fears, the doubts, the tears, the frustrations, the impatience, the faith, the…

That was it! It all made sense. For some reason, yet unrevealed, I was being blessed with the opportunity to know the limitless bounds of true faith, to trust on a very deep level that somehow my challenges would, indeed, serve some greater purpose, that it was part of God's plan for my life. I only needed to do my best along the way, to ignore those who didn't understand or who were judgmental, and to draw on the power of my faith. I needed to be patient.

I needed to be RESILIENT.

PILLAR #1

Define your situation.

"I can be changed by what happens to me. But I refuse to be reduced by it."

Maya Angelou

Since that fateful day in 1994, and over the years and challenges that followed, people would ask me, "How did you get through that?" When I sat down to write this book, I realized that I rely on certain characteristics and habits whenever I'm faced with a challenge or crisis. I call these my "5 Pillars" and I'll share them throughout the book.

Pillar #1: Define your situation.

Nothing in my life was the same after I was assaulted. Nor would it ever be the same again. "Normal" life was a thing of past. I had to discover a new normal.

I couldn't work. I had no income, no way to support myself. But I had to go to physical therapy appointments. I had counseling appointments with a therapist to deal with the post-traumatic stress. Thankfully I was put on disability (which I had to pay back to the airline with my first three months of checks once I returned to duty).

It would have been easy to give up. But being the determined so-and-so that I am, I believed that this was happening for a reason, and I that could and would make a life for myself no matter what. So, I made a plan.

I think of this like assessing the damage after a storm. Once the storm is over, you can step outside and look at the debris and create a plan to clean up and repair anything that was broken.

Likewise, once the emergency of a crisis situation has settled down, you can calmly and clearly survey the aspects of your life both physical (health and home) and financial (your job and insurance).

Here are some questions to get you started in defining your situation:
- What is it that you are coming back from?
- What are the challenges that lie ahead?
- How can you meet those challenges?
- What resources are available to you?

Literally sit down and write all of this out (I talk more about keeping a journal in Pillar #2). Then make your comeback plan. Prioritize what's most important and create goals for accomplishing your plan.

When I had my first brain tumor surgery, I was a physical wreck. I made list of what faculties I had lost (like my speech, eyesight, and balance—I'm deaf in my right ear, so my balance will be funky forever) and what I wanted to work on, and progress goals. I shared these with my physical therapist so she could incorporate what I wanted into her treatment and care plan.

Asking for help

Let me be clear about something: *you do not have to do any of this alone*. I didn't always feel this way. What's interesting is how I evolved from crisis to crisis. At first, after my assault, I was insistent on doing everything myself, not asking anyone for help. I'm a little stubborn that way. In hindsight, though, this isn't the best or only option.

After my first brain tumor some 16 years later, however, my stance against asking for help had softened dramatically. I couldn't drive myself anywhere; heck, I had to learn to speak again for heaven's sake! I had to get to physical therapy appointments and go grocery shopping. So, I reached out and asked for help with these basics. And you know what? Help was not only forthcoming, but people *wanted* to help.

So, if you're like me (the old me) and you don't like asking for help, be kind to yourself especially if you're in crisis mode or recovering from a crisis. Be open to asking for help. Feel and express your gratitude for it. And then commit to paying it forward later when you're stronger.

4

Back on my feet

I knew I needed to be resilient, but I also needed a job. Fast. And I needed a good job, one that would generate enough income to provide me with financial stability and long-term opportunity.

My ongoing health challenges precluded me from many positions for which I was otherwise qualified. I never knew if I were going to have a good day or a bad day health-wise. I wasn't in a position to take on full-time employment, nor to work in an environment that in any way was demanding on my body, including a long commute from my home in Mission Viejo; sitting in a car for long periods was physically brutal and mentally draining. Not happening.

Telecommuting was just starting to gain traction in the late 1990s/early 2000. California led the way nationwide, due to its love affair with technology rooted in Silicon Valley in the north. And in the south, it was prompted by the horrific commute times, skyrocketing gasoline prices, and resultant air pollution that were all rampant in southern California, and particularly in Orange County where I lived.

It seemed that telecommuting might be a viable option, given my particular set of circumstances, and I started thinking about how to generate a career within the parameters of working from home.

Instead of trying to craft a solution, the solution literally just came to me. I have no doubt that God was guiding my next steps, they unfolded so effortlessly. It seemed my prayers were being answered, without my having formulated exactly what I needed. Awesome how God does that, isn't it?

You see, while I had been working at Southwest, I had often been asked by professional athletes I had met through our family's friendship with Jeff Newman and his teammates to help with event planning for charity events or non-profit organization parties — golf tournaments, galas, celebrity auctions, etc. It's not that I had experience with event planning, they thought it was something I could do. I'll chalk it up to divine intervention once more.

I have no doubt that God was guiding my next steps, they unfolded so effortlessly.

I enjoyed the work, using marketing and organizational skills to help others make a difference. My networking among sports and entertainment personalities had grown organically, and I was more than happy to facilitate connecting high visibility people with common philanthropic interests and goals. After all, these folks had the financial means to help a lot of people.

Other than the actual event itself, most of the work was accomplished on the phone or on the computer. As the opportunities continued to come to me unsolicited, I realized that my skill set was ideal for this type of work, so I carved out a niche for myself as an independent contractor doing event planning. I focused primarily on charity and non-profit foundation work. I learned a lot about the inner workings of

In 2006, I traveled to New Orleans with a non-profit doing outreach in the 9th Ward after Hurricane Katrina.

non-profit organizations when I worked with their representatives. Unbeknownst to me at time, this knowledge would serve me well in the future.

That said, with my burgeoning new career, I felt it was incumbent upon me to be as informed as possible (back to the "if you can't do it right, don't do it at all" adage!), so in 2000, I returned to the University of California at Irvine and completed its certification program in non-profits and fundraising. It was important to me that I was solid with industry knowledge, not just qualified based on my experiential expertise. The desired snowball effect happened on its own, and work was steady.

Though I enjoyed the actual event planning work itself, I was motivated by helping others; it was never "just a job" for me. That's always been important to me; I grew up in a household that instilled the value of donating time and effort to help others. For example, when I was a teenager, Mom voluntarily spent time with cancer patients in the local hospital, helping the families in any way she could, providing what amounted to hospice services to terminally ill friends and neighbors before it was called "hospice." Frequently, she took me along.

That experience had a profound impact on my life. During my rehabilitation after my assault, I started volunteering with Southwest's chosen charity, Ronald McDonald House. We would go to the children's hospital in Orange County and read books or go for walks with the kids. Many of them were alone much of the time as their parents worked during the day. Few parents can afford to take time off when their child is undergoing a lengthy medical treatment or rehabilitation.

I started a non-profit called Angels Within in 1996, as I wanted to expand beyond Orange County and take volunteers into different hospitals and pediatric wards. I recruited volunteers to go into the hospitals for reading, game days, or just watching TV with the kids. I brought in entertainment and celebrities, too, to meet the kids.

Unlike most non-profits, the organization did not solicit funds, it asked only for commitments of time. I think it's fair to say that those who participated received as much benefit as they provided.

Little did I know back then how deeply the seeds of helping others were planted; and how the landscape of my later life would be affected by those very solid roots.

5

My rock crumbles

Everyone who knows me, knows that my dad was my hero, and I was his "Nels." I believe that our closeness was borne at least in small part from the fact that he was so much older when he became a dad. Not many 45-year old men were first-time fathers in 1967.

My mom always seemed to understand the special bond my dad and I had. Instead of resenting it, as so many mothers do in that situation, she appreciated his dedication and unfettered demonstrations of love toward me. Mom was secure of his love in their marriage, and being mindful that they had gotten a later start in life together, she didn't waste even a moment on feelings of jealousy or resentment toward me. I was incredibly fortunate to have an abundance of love from both parents, and have always considered myself extremely blessed to have been raised by Bob and Carol Nelson, no question.

I was also blessed to have a loving home at which to stay while I was recovering from my injuries. Our family home in Mission Viejo was large enough to afford privacy for all three adults in the house, while cozy enough to feel safe and nurturing.

One afternoon in early March 2001, I was resting on the den sofa after having had a particularly intensive physical therapy appointment earlier in the day. My parents were at a local outpatient clinic for my dad's colonoscopy, part of his annual physical. Now almost 79 years old, he had always been mindful about the need to stay in the best health possible, and that included regular check-ups.

I had no reason to think that today's appointment would be any different than other years, so I barely looked up as my parents came through the door; I was involved with a TV show blaring from the corner of the den. My father softly called my name, and something in his voice immediately alerted me that something was very, very wrong. My heart started beating even more wildly when I turned and saw the look on my mother's face. I braced myself for what I knew was going to be news I did *not* want to hear.

My dad walked over to me, his 6'8" strides quickly closing the gap from the doorway to the sofa, and he sat down. Calmly and matter-of-factly, as a true Norwegian descendant would be, my dad spoke. He was tightly clutching my outstretched hand, silently willing me to be strong.

"So, the doctor found a few polyps today, and because they didn't look quite right, he had them biopsied right away. The biopsy showed there were malignant cells present; I've got colon cancer, Nels."

My world stopped at that moment. Literally. It was as if there were some magic trick, where everyone was suspended mid-sentence, mid-gesturing. Then, I felt like I was under water, unable to breathe, unable to think clearly, everything in slow motion.

My dad, always so tall, so strong, my rock, my everything; and cancer. It was inconceivable to me. Colon cancer? Not my dad! There had to be some mistake! Mistakes were made in labs all the time! This simply could not be! The doctor was wrong! The doctor *had* to be wrong! Tears welled up in my eyes, but no words came out, as my mind raced, trying to come up for some other explanation for the biopsy results than the truth I did not want to hear—and could not accept.

My dad was still talking, so I tried to focus on what he was saying.

"I need to go in the hospital right away, tomorrow, and they're going to do surgery. It looks like the cancer is confined to a local area; they'll know more after they go in. I'm going to be fine, Nels, no worries. I'm going to be fine," he said, mustering a smile.

My mom had come up behind him at that point, and she reached down and held me tightly. She pulled back and took my face in her hands, and bravely put a smile on her face to match my father's.

"Annie? We can get through this. They caught it early, and you know your dad is strong. He's going to be okay. You know he wouldn't leave his girls," she said, looking over at him, and he nodded in assent.

I wiped the tears that were threatening to spill down my face and took a deep breath, inwardly praying that my father would be okay—he just *had* to be okay, right?—while fighting the fear he would not. But at that moment, my focus necessarily shifted to my dad, and I summoned the inner strength to say what I knew he both needed and wanted me to say at that moment. After all, I have Norwegian blood in my veins, too.

"Ok. I'm ok. You're right. We can do this. We *will* do this. We will. We must. God will provide."

Recovery, delayed

The surgery to remove the malignant cells in Dad's colon was successful. The cancer had, indeed, been contained, so he did not need radiation or chemotherapy afterwards. We were encouraged at the good report immediately following surgery, and though the procedure had taken a lot out of my elderly father, the consensus was that he was going to be okay.

But my dad wasn't okay. Lying in his hospital bed after the colon cancer surgery, my dad's back pain became unbearable, more than would be expected under the circumstances. Then, he spiked a significant fever; he could barely move. Dad was quickly moved to ICU, as the doctors began running tests to determine what else was going on. The tests confirmed what the doctors had suspected: my father had contracted a staph infection in the hospital that had invaded his spine, centered in the two vertebrae in his back that had been damaged in a fall three years earlier. The staph infection further depleted the weakened vertebra. He was administered fluids, antibiotics, and was sedated for the excruciating pain.

For 39 days, my father was in ICU, battling the insidious and unrelenting staph infection. My mother and I stayed by his side around the clock, I took the day shift while she worked as a real estate agent, and she took the night shift. Finally, Dad was moved out of ICU to a private room, and we continued our round-the-clock routine as he continued to fight against the staph that had invaded his back. He gradually gained enough strength to come home in early September, more than five months after his colon cancer surgery.

We set up a hospital bed in the den so that he could look out at the gardens in the backyard. He was frail, weak, and in need of I.V. therapy at the house, but we settled into a routine to get him back on his feet. What mattered was that after five long months, he was finally home. Everything was going to be okay. Life would start getting back to normal now.

Or, so we thought.

A shaken nation, and more bad news

Shortly before 6:00 a.m. (Pacific Standard Time) on the morning of September 11, 2001, I was just waking up. As was my habit, I somewhat absentmindedly turned on the TV. I started to head toward the bathroom, but the visual on the screen paralyzed me. I just stood there in the middle of my bedroom, transfixed, staring at the TV, which was filled with frantic, loud coverage of the first Twin Tower having just been hit. Then, shaking out of my reverie like a sudden shattering of glass, I raced down the stairs to where my parents were—my mom in the bedroom, my father in the hospital bed we had set up in the den when he came home. I was screaming as I ran, "Turn on the TV! Turn on the TV!" Almost instantly, we witnessed in horror, along with the rest of the world, the live footage of another plane hitting the second Twin Tower.

For the remainder of the day, we sat in front of the television, unable to articulate our brain-numbing thoughts, as most people were wont to do that day. There were no words; there simply were no words. As more reports poured in, fears of other terror attacks were confirmed when news the

Pentagon was hit, and then the crash of Flight 93 near Shanksville, Pennsylvania, came across the airwaves.

Horrible image upon horrible image continuously flashed across the screen, each one more abominable than the one before: the collapse of the Twin Towers; the chaos at the Pentagon; the huge crater from Flight 93's impact into the soft, early morning Pennsylvania farmland; mangled buildings and broken bodies; fires, emergency sirens, and worse. Veteran news broadcasters struggled to keep their composure on camera, in utter disbelief at the overwhelming flow of information which their job dictated they share with the viewing audience. The federal government quickly and swiftly issued safety mandates, including grounding all planes in U.S. airspace, an unprecedented move that had never happened before, nor has happened since. The President spoke to a shaken nation.

Though my parents and I were safe in my childhood home in California, our country's safety had been shattered in the span of less than 90 minutes. It was unthinkable. And ultimately, for many, it was a call to action—including me.

Over the course of the next few months after 9/11, I often prayed about how to help. I loved our country and knew there had to be something I could do to make a difference, but out of necessity during that time, my day-to-day focus was still my father. From September through the end of the year, my mother and I nursed him back to better health. Not good health; better health. Still, something seemed "off."

By early January 2002, though Dad had never fully regained his former good color, nor enough weight on his tall, lanky frame, his spirits were definitely lifted when he and my mom decided to go to Arizona for an extended visit. Dad loved it there, and at that point, anything that made Dad happy was good by me, even though selfishly I didn't want him to go. As I waved good-bye to my parents from our driveway in Mission Viejo, I promised to join them over the upcoming weekend.

Understandably, the trip to Arizona wiped Dad out. He pretty much stayed in bed the first few days after arriving. When I drove to visit the first weekend as promised, he was still in bed most of the time. Mom and I were both concerned. He seemed so frail, so weak. I was hesitant to go back to California at the end of the weekend, but Dad assured me he was fine, and I uneasily made plans to visit again in two weeks.

After a few more days, when my father still was clearly not feeling well, Mom took him to a doctor in Phoenix. The news was not good. They suspected he had cancer again, this time in the lung.

My parents did not call me that first night. Typically, they did not want to worry me unless they had something definitive to tell. While Dad slept soundly from exhaustion, Mom got up and paced through their place in the semi-darkness, her mind going through all the options, mulling over every possibility. Shortly after midnight, she made up her mind what to do. Come what may, Mom was going to make sure that Dad got the best medical care possible.

The Mayo Clinic had opened a hospital in Scottsdale in 1998, and Mom managed to get the phone number of its Oncology Department. Predictably, since it was the middle of the night, she got an answering machine. Mom left a heartfelt, lengthy message about Dad's medical history and the current suspicion he had cancer yet again. She tried unsuccessfully to hold back the tears during the message, and then hung up.

Imagine my mother's surprise when the phone rang at 6:30 a.m. the next morning, and she found herself talking to the Head of the Mayo Clinic's Oncology Department! The doctor had come in early that day and had picked up the phone message himself—divine intervention, if ever there were any—and he told her that he had been very moved by what she had said.

He then asked, "Can you bring your husband into the clinic this morning at 10:30?"

My mother assured the doctor she could, and hung up in disbelief and gratitude. Her impassioned plea for the husband she had loved for 38 years had worked.

Mom and Dad arrived well ahead of the scheduled appointment time and were immediately ushered into the first of many medical rooms Dad would visit that day. After an all-day regimen of being examined and providing pertinent medical background information, bloodwork, x-rays, and more, they went home and had a nice dinner together, before falling asleep in one another's arms.

The next day, the doctor met with my parents to share the results of my dad's tests. The news was grim. My father had primary lung cancer, it was fast-growing—and it was inoperable. The doctor then honestly and gently discussed the pros and cons of chemotherapy, making it clear that, while chemotherapy might prolong his life, it would not cure my dad's cancer; he was terminal. At this point, it was a matter of "when" and not "if." Chemo would only buy him a little more time.

Dad looked at Mom and took a deep breath, seeking her input. "This is your decision, Bob," she said, holding back the tears. "I'll support whatever choice you make."

Dad sat for a moment, but only a brief moment, looking out the window. He then turned to the doctor with great resolve and said, "I'll try it for my girls."

I got the call later that evening, after my parents had arrived back home. To say I was devastated would be a gross understatement. My heart, literally, hurt. I held it together pretty well on the phone, but after I hung up, I collapsed on the floor, hysterical. My father was going to die; and there was nothing anyone could do about it.

I don't know how long I sat on the floor, but the sun had long-since set when I finally found the strength to stand and walk through the dark house to the bathroom. I flipped the light switch and turned on the faucet. Using my hands, I scooped icy cold water onto my face a few times, then slowly looked at myself in the mirror, the water dripping onto the counter, the four light bulbs stretching across the top edge of the mirror casting me in a distorted light. Standing there, I asked my reflection aloud how I could face the world without my dad; my hero; my best friend? But the only reply was massive tears flowing down my face.

Then, looking upward, my heart breaking for our family, I asked God, "How much more could we take?"

The tenderest gesture

Anyone who has gone through, or witnessed a loved one go through, chemotherapy understands that the process is at least as bad as the disease. And unfortunately, like many people, my dad did not do well with his first round of treatment. He was still so weak from the colon cancer and staph infection that his capacity to handle the devastating impact of radiation and chemotherapy was almost nil.

I drove to Arizona from Mission Viejo every third day for the first few weeks after his diagnosis, but soon made the decision to stay with my parents for whatever time we had left together. After starting the second round of chemo, Dad had a "quantity vs. quality of life" talk with the doctor and opted to halt all treatment, to enjoy whatever time he had left with "his girls."

Winter quickly turned to spring, spring turned to early summer, and the summer months passed. I noticed Dad was sleeping more as time went on, but his mental faculties remained amazingly acute. He kept his natural good humor, and enjoyed spending time with family and friends, including my friend, Lisa, who was also living in Arizona. Dad always brightened when Lisa stopped by, whether she was alone, or with her children.

The days unfolded fairly predictably, one day pretty much like any other, except for the occasional trip to the doctor. But on Wednesday, September 4 as Dad and I sat in the kitchen, he whispered urgently to me while glancing at Mom, who was watching TV in the den.

"I need you to take me to Wal-Mart," he said. I protested, surely anything he needed I could go and get for him? And Wal-Mart? Really?

"No, I need to go," he insisted. "I need you to take me to Wal-Mart. *Today*. Now, please. And please don't tell your mother where we're going."

Not one to argue with my father, especially when he was so ill, I agreed. We got up from the kitchen table and slowly headed toward the front door. As we were crossing the den, Mom raised her eyebrows at me questioningly. I said something vague about going out for a little bit as I ever-so-slightly shook my head, and she smiled, told us to have a good time, and nonchalantly looked back toward the TV. I helped Dad into my parents' white Chevy Trailblazer and we drove to Wal-Mart as he had asked.

We pulled into the handicapped space in front of the store and I automatically reached for the handicap placard for the mirror, as I had done many times over the past year. Next, I climbed out of the car, opened the back hatch, and grabbed the folded-up walker. At this point, I was deft in setting the walker up for my father's tall frame, and I quickly snapped it into place.

I pushed the walker to the passenger door, and my heart ached as I helped Dad ease out of the car. His movements were slow and deliberate. He was clearly in pain, but he was also fiercely determined. We walked together with measured steps into the store, and I carefully supported him beneath his arms, as I lowered him gingerly onto one of the courtesy wheelchairs. I still had no idea what Dad wanted at Wal-Mart, or why it was so important that he was physically there — he had been quiet in the car — but it clearly was important to him.

"Where to, Dad?" I asked, trying to keep my tone light, as I wheeled him past the official Wal-Mart door greeter toward the myriad of shelves filled with every conceivable product you could need (and many more you might not).

"There," he said, gesturing to the greeting card department.

I wheeled Dad over to the greeting cards, and for the next 30 minutes he carefully read, rejected, and finally selected, cards for every occasion: birthday, anniversary, and blank cards that could be used for holidays. It was all I could do to keep from weeping in the aisle, as he handed the chosen cards to me, one-by-one. Finally satisfied, he was ready to go.

As we pulled up in front of the house, Dad reached for my hand and smiled. "Don't turn the car off, just yet, Nels. Hand me the cards, please. Do you have a pen?"

I grabbed the small bag from the back seat, fished a pen out of my purse, and obediently handed everything over to him. As we sat in the running car, Dad proceeded to write to my mom on each card. He wanted her to have a card from him for every special occasion the first year he was gone, knowing that the first year would be the hardest.

I looked away while Dad was writing and held back the tears, overwhelmed by witnessing this thoughtful gesture of gentle kindness that had always defined my dad. Here he was, close to his death, and yet his focus was on making sure that my mom was going to be ok the first year he was gone. A man of deep faith, he had no fears about dying, he knew he would soon join our Lord, but he both wanted and needed my mom to know that he would be with her still.

After writing each of the cards and sealing the envelopes, he handed them to me.

"Annie, I need you to make sure your mom gets these. And there's one more thing I need you to promise that you will do for me. Promise me," he said, looking directly into my eyes, serious as I had ever seen him.

"Anything, Dad, you know that," I said, bracing myself for his request, knowing it was going to tear at my heart.

"Every year on your mom's and my anniversary," he said slowly, "until she marries again, or falls in love with someone else, I want you to send her a dozen yellow roses from me."

I could only nod my head, no words came out, but my eyes filled with tears.

"Ok," he said, smiling, "let's get in the house, your mother will wonder what we're doing sitting out here in the car."

I placed the sealed cards in my purse and helped Dad into the house, settling him into bed for a much-needed nap. He quickly fell into a deep, contented sleep, as I sat next to him, grateful for every breath he still took.

Saying goodbye

The day after our trip to Wal-Mart, the next-door neighbors stopped by for a visit. I took note of the fact that Dad politely cut it a little short, which was somewhat unusual, but the rest of the day was pretty normal. Friday morning, Dad was in the kitchen feeding my dog, Pumpkin, a banana. Pumpkin was a Rhodesian Ridgeback, and at seven years of age, she had been my constant companion since my assault. I had lunch plans with my friend Lisa that day, so I had arranged for the hospice nurse to come by while I was out, to help Mom support Dad with anything he might need.

Before I arrived at Lisa's, Mom called and said that the hospice nurse felt it was time — Dad was about to pass away. I immediately whipped the car into the nearest driveway, turned the car around, and gunned it down the road back to my parents' house. On the way, I called the minister and asked him to meet me at the house.

As I ran in the door, the nurse was pulling the hospital bed away from the wall in the master bedroom, making it more accessible: Dad was adamant that he did not want to die in their marital bed, he did not want Mom to have that memory. I used the wheelchair to move Dad to the hospital bed from their bedroom —

he was too weak to walk that short distance — and I got him settled in, just as Mom answered the door to the minister.

Dad laid there with his eyes closed. As the minister stepped toward the hospital bed, Dad woke up and greeted the minister. We all retreated slightly, that Dad might have privacy to speak. After a few minutes, Dad peacefully drifted off to sleep. The minister looked at us quizzically, so Mom followed him outside.

A few minutes later, Mom came back into the house and she was literally shaking. Incredibly, she and the minister had had an argument. He had insisted it was clearly *not* my dad's time, because Dad "didn't look that bad," plus he was totally coherent. Hearing that, the three of us — the nurse, Mom, and I — looked at one another in surprise. That certainly wasn't what all of us felt! Yet, from across the room, Dad's breaths continued slowly and steadily. The nurse left shortly thereafter, with instructions to call if there were any change in his condition.

That night, Mom and I slept in the master bedroom (with Pumpkin, of course) in case Dad needed anything, but he slept through the night. The next morning, Saturday, September 7, I was awakened by the sound of Dad's labored breathing. The fluid from the cancer was slowly filling his lungs, and he was struggling to breathe. We took turns sitting next to him as each of us got ready for the day. The hospice nurse arrived soon after, checked his vitals, and left shortly thereafter. For the next several hours, Mom and I rotated Dad in the bed to help with the increasing build-up of fluid in his lungs. By then, he was fairly incoherent, and we did everything possible to make him comfortable.

I had called Lisa the night before and had tearfully filled her in on Dad's deteriorating condition, so later that morning, it came as no surprise when the doorbell rang, and there she stood with her then-7-year old daughter, Ashley. Lisa hugged me tightly, as Ashley ran past us both and jumped onto Dad's hospital bed.

"Hi, Grandpa Bob!" she said cheerily, smiling and reaching over to plant a sweet kiss on his cheek, unaware as only an innocent child can be that Dad's time with us was assuredly coming to an end.

Dad opened his eyes and his face lit up at seeing Ashley.

"Hi, Ash!" he said, in a scratchy, whispered voice, and then his eyes closed again.

Ashley gave him another quick kiss and climbed down off the bed. She went to the family room, where my mom was sitting on the sofa, snuggled next to Mom and quietly focused on her coloring book. Lisa and I stayed at Dad's bedside. Though he would periodically open and close his eyes, he never spoke again after greeting Ashley. Lisa had the opportunity to say her good-bye, and they left shortly thereafter.

Mom and I sat with Dad for the next several hours. When it seemed he could hear us, I gently said, "Show me those baby blues, Dad." And he did — opening his beautiful eyes for a brief moment, before closing them again, the effort to keep his eyes open far too difficult.

As the afternoon wore on, our dear friends Art and Theresa Engelen came over, so that Mom and I were not alone during those final few hours. As early evening came and the sun began to set, Dad's breathing became even more labored. Mom and I were sitting on either side of him, each of us holding his hand, as Art and Theresa stood nearby. Suddenly, he emitted a sound

—not the death rattle you hear about, but a loud sound that I had never heard before. Instinctively, I knew what it meant. I jumped up from the bed and raced from the room, suddenly unable to face truly saying good-bye.

Art knew me well, and he understood my inability to face those final moments; but he also knew that if I didn't say good-bye to my father, it was something I would regret for the rest of my life—and Art was right. He followed me into the other room and spoke to me in an urgent, authoritative voice, thankfully breaking through my overwhelming emotions, and I quickly came back to where my dad lay, dying. Mom stepped aside as I leaned down and buried my face in my father's neck, telling him I loved him, tearfully saying good-bye. He let me know he had heard me; and then he drew his last breath.

Dad was gone; and a part of Mom and me died that day, too.

6

And now this

We had two services for Dad, one in Arizona in mid-September, and another in Mission Viejo two weeks later, on September 29. At his first service, I wanted to honor Dad by giving his eulogy. Standing before family and friends, I somehow managed to share what an amazing man he had been without dissolving into tears, as Mom sat stoically in the front row, lost in her own thoughts about the man she had loved long and happily.

After the services, everyone came back to my parents' house and we had a big Italian dinner, complete with an open bar. As the sun was waning, we all walked to the golf course behind the house and stood in a circle, as each person relayed a special story about my father. The last person finished speaking just as the sun slowly set over the horizon, perfectly aligned with the "setting sun" of Dad's life. My father's services were truly a celebration of his time here with us, beautifully reflected in the abundant love that overflowed from those attending.

The services in Mission Viejo were held in the Elks Lodge where Dad had been a member for many years. Rev. Robert Schuler, Jr., our long-time pastor, officiated. Every seat was taken with people paying their last respects. The outpouring of support from family and friends truly helped get us through those difficult times. Mom and I could not have made it without the overwhelming thoughtfulness and kindness of so many.

But, that said, it was clear to see that the previous two years had taken their toll on my 64-year old mother. She was always exhausted, and had had a cough that never quite went away. Her color was not good. Before Dad passed away (and despite her best efforts), he could see that oftentimes — too often, actually — she wasn't feeling well, so shortly before his death, he made her promise that she would have a physical.

Two weeks after the Mission Viejo services, Mom honored her promise to Dad and saw the cardiologist who had been treating her for years, Dr. Jacob. She went through two days of diagnostic tests. The third day, late on a Friday afternoon, she and I went to meet with the doctor for the results. We walked in, said hello, took the two seats in front of his desk, and waited for him to begin.

> *It was clear to see that the previous two years had taken their toll on my 64-year old mother.*

I felt slightly alarmed as Dr. Jacob sat there. He looked perplexed. After glancing at Mom's test results spread out on the desk in front of him, he started to speak, hesitated, and then told us that despite the fact all of her tests seemed normal, he just felt something was wrong. While we were sitting there, Dr. Jacob informally called another doctor into his office and showed him Mom's results. The second doctor looked over the file, and he concurred that everything looked fine. But Dr. Jacob still was not comfortable, so he had Mom step across the hall for a chest x-ray, and told us to come back on Monday for the results.

The x-ray technician took the typical chest views, then asked Mom to wait a few moments so she could check the films. Attempting a smile, the tech came back into the room and somewhat apologetically said she needed to take a few more x-rays, from different angles.

Mom knew from experience that that meant the tech had found something suspicious—but, of course, the woman couldn't say anything. Meanwhile, I was sitting in the hallway, and as time dragged on, I started wondering what was taking so long. A sense of uneasiness was washing over me, which I successfully pushed from my mind. Everything was fine, and the x-ray was going to prove just that: Everything was *fine*.

A few minutes later, as Mom and I headed down the hallway to leave the building, mundanely deciding where to go for dinner, the x-ray tech rushed up behind us and said that Dr. Jacob wanted to see her. Like, now. Mom politely disagreed, saying that the tech must be mistaken because she had an appointment on Monday morning to go over the results with him. But the tech insisted the doctor wanted to see Mom right away, so with great trepidation—it's never good news when they want to see you that quickly—we turned around and walked down the long corridor that led back to Dr. Jacob's office.

Entering his office, my heart stopped when I saw his face. He was clearly upset with what he was going to have to tell his long-time patient. I said a silent prayer for strength and braced myself, glancing over at Mom. She took a deep breath and encouraged him with a smile, but he was looking down, as if trying to think how he wanted to tell her what was surely bad news.

"And?" Mom finally asked gently, breaking the awkward silence.

"Mrs. Nelson, we have a problem," he said, as he looked up, a few tears slowing spilling over, falling down his face. Mom didn't hesitate a whit in response.

"So ... I have cancer?" she asked, matter-of-factly.

"I'm afraid you might," he said, quietly. "You have a rare tumor called a 'thymoma,' which is pressing against your aortic valve. It looks like it's affecting your lung, too. We need to biopsy the tumor to find out what we're dealing with, and if it's malignant, you're going to need surgery."

Dr. Jacob immediately put Mom in the hospital, and the next day he biopsied the tumor, which revealed that there were malignant cells present. Mom's surgery took place within a week, and only six weeks after Dad's death. She was fortunate that the cancer was contained within the tumor; she did not need radiation or chemotherapy. Still, the surgery itself was very invasive, and her recovery was understandably lengthy.

To be honest, that time is pretty much a blur to me; together, Mom and I got through it. In retrospect, I suppose there isn't much choice but to do what must be done when confronted with life challenges that threaten to overwhelm you.

It's only after a crisis has passed that you have the "luxury" to examine the emotional aspect of the experiences. At the time, the survival mechanism kicks in, and somehow you get through things you never thought you could. That doesn't mean it doesn't come at a cost (and sometimes a high cost), but still, you do—because you must.

But I also have to point out that there was—as there always is—a blessing in the timing of how things unfolded. Simply put, after Dad died, Mom needed me. My focus, out of necessity, was on the living. I had to concentrate on the present; I had to look forward, not back. I know Dad would have wanted that. And because Mom and I only had each other, we quickly bonded in a very special way not only over Dad's death, but also over Mom's life.

> *It's only after a crisis has passed that you have the "luxury" to examine the emotional aspect of the experiences.*

Ultimately, because of Mom's cancer, I found inner strength to fight for her; and Mom fought for life, because of me.

Mom recuperated in Mission Viejo through the Christmas holidays and then returned to Arizona. Her favorite memories of Dad were there for her, just as my most cherished memories of our time together were in California. I went with Mom to Arizona at the beginning of the New Year to help her until she was fully back on her feet, and for the next months in early 2003, I visited her on a regular basis.

For the remainder of 2003, I continued to focus on my event planning business, which was growing exponentially. But despite the commercial success, for which I was humbled and grateful, I likewise was deeply disturbed by the then-current events.

And, as happens when you are uncomfortable in a situation, you don't stand idly by and continue living with the discomfort—you do something about it.

PILLAR #2

Make a personal inventory.

"The meaning of life is to find your
gift. The purpose of life
is to give it away."

Pablo Picasso

Pillar #2: Take a personal inventory.

For most of us, a crisis is a wake-up call. When you come out the other side of a crisis, you'll want to make the most of your time.

You'll take less for granted. You'll want to live with purpose and be truly happy.

You'll realize that punching a clock day after boring day is a waste of your precious time without something more. You'll want to better yourself—and others, too.

It may take a lot of soul searching to find "the thing" that will feel like your calling, that will bring meaning and purpose into your life.

For me, that soul searching included taking an inventory of myself after I left the airline and found myself without a job, and without the ability to take a regular 8-to-5 job because of my inconsistent health.

I sat down and thought, who am I? What are my best traits? What am I great at? What are my gifts? What comes naturally and easily to me?

For me that including performing, public speaking, being in front of people. I was photogenic and creative.

As I sat with my list (and, yes, prayed about it), the natural answer emerged, which was to start my own business (I could work around my health) as an event planner. For you, the answer will be completely different.

Keeping a journal

After my assault on the airplane, I sought help from my pastor and psychologists for my post traumatic stress. They all recommended keeping a journal.

When you write out your thoughts, feelings and emotions, it will trigger more thoughts and ideas. Through journaling and exploring my thoughts, I found the triggers for my anxiety which allowed me to look at them and heal them. All the answers were inside me, and they all flowed out as an expression of myself through journaling.

If you've gone through (or are going through) a crisis and you've never journaled before, give this a try. Your journal doesn't have to be fancy — just a notebook from the drugstore and a pen is all you need.

I know there are phone apps that claim to be journals, but trust me on this: there is power in using your hands to *write out* your thoughts and feelings. Something happens between the brain and the hands and the paper.

So, go to the dollar store or drugstore and pick up a notebook. Some people like fat lines, some like skinny lines, and others prefer no lines so they can draw and doodle along with writing.

It might feel awkward at first, or you might feel like you're just rambling, but go with it. Let out whatever wants and needs to come out. Trust me. Just do it. Something magnificent will emerge.

7

Finding my mission

To understand what happened in my life beginning in 2004 (and continuing to this day), it's important to go back in time and remember the constellation of circumstances that were occurring in the world back then, because those very circumstances influenced, shaped, and dramatically changed my world in a way that I could never have foreseen.

In response to the 9/11 terrorist attack, the U.S. had invaded Afghanistan, beginning "Operation Enduring Freedom" on October 7, 2001, alongside military forces from the United Kingdom and Afghanistan. Devastating news reports about the war were headline news in the media every single day. Our military forces in Afghanistan were soon joined by military support from 57 other nations.

By 2003, the War in Afghanistan was raging, when another battlefront began in Iraq, "Operation Iraqi Freedom." Initially fought by the U.S., U.K., Australia, and Poland, 36 other countries soon joined the multinational forces in Iraq.

News reports of the intense battles in both countries continued to dominate the airwaves in 2003 and 2004. Everyday Americans rushed to look up the location of cities across the globe that most had never heard of before — Kabul, Kandahar Province, Jalalabad, Baghdad, Kirkuk, Tikrit and Fallujah. Words and names that had initially seemed strange to us became household words: Taliban, al Qaeda, Mujahideen,

Saddam Hussein, Osama bin Laden, and more. The world stage was dominated by the agendas of religious zealots and extremists, bent on waging a "holy war" on the "heathen infidels" — us.

Our brave men and women in uniform serving in Afghanistan and Iraq were fighting for America's freedom, and many sacrificed their lives. As the troops were putting their lives on the line under horrific conditions in Afghanistan and Iraq, back home in the U.S. there was ongoing intellectual and political debate over the necessity of the wars, the funding of the wars, and the justification of the wars. Our country was severely divided over these issues — and still is. Anger flared on both sides, with finger-pointing, shouting, and demonstrations.

For me personally, I resoundingly came down on the side of supporting those serving in our military. I still do. I have never understood, then or now, why people who so passionately embrace and employ their freedom of speech in order to disagree, nonetheless resist understanding and appreciating that their very right to disagree is *because* of those who fight for that freedom to express their opinions, *regardless* of the content of those opinions! It seems to me that their ingratitude is insulting to those who make the choice to maintain our country's freedoms for everyone.

That's not a "soapbox thought." To me, it's pure common sense. The troops don't sit around the barracks and have a debate about the whys and wherefores of fighting before going into battle. They train hard to do their job; they do their job and it's a job not many want — less than one percent of the U.S. population serves in its all-volunteer military.

And then when they come home, they shoulder the many burdens of service — like dealing with PTS and TBI (traumatic brain injury)—after performing their job that non-serving people in our country do not and cannot understand.

Unlike other wonderful, helping professions like law enforcement, educators, first responders the medical community to name a few, the military is unique in that their "workforce" is for the benefit of the entire world, not just our country or not a segment of our country, or a city, or a town, or even an individual. They work for all of us, all over the world, and they deserve our support, as well as our gratitude for their courage, dedication, and willingness to sacrifice, as do their families.

Given the deep and heartfelt emotions I've just shared, I'm sure it's clear that military service has always been something I have highly valued, as has my family. My father was not able to serve because at 6'8", he was too tall. Dad never truly got over his inability to make that contribution; he spoke of it often as I grew up. His father, a Norwegian citizen (he's the grandpa on whose birthday I had been born) served with the U.S. military as part of the Normandy Beach Invasion. My mother's brothers were both in the U.S. Army. Yet those I knew who had served never talked about their service. So, though I was raised respecting the military, I knew nothing about actual military service, and I had no idea how to show my appreciation to those serving.

But watching the news broadcasts about Afghanistan and Iraq, and with a strong sense of patriotism, I grew more and more impatient with myself. I was not content to stand by and watch from the sidelines, I wanted to actually "do" something. I was obviously not physically capable of actively serving, and with that thought I understood in some small measure what Dad must have felt when he could not actively serve. I was vocal in sharing my thoughts supporting the military, but that seemed somewhat benign and not directly beneficial to anyone serving. So, over the course of a few months, though I mulled over ideas, none seemed to be right; none seemed to be *enough*. There had to be something hands-on to do, but what?

Message received!

While contemplating my course of action, I finally decided to go through the personal effects that Dad had left to me. I was ready to enjoy the possessions of his which he wanted me to have, without falling apart for the reason I had them.

I walked downstairs to the guestroom closet and reached on the top shelf for the old, hard-sided brown suitcase, its brass hinges firmly locked. Placing it on the bed, I carefully pressed outwardly on the two small brass squares that were positioned next to the hinges, and the hinges flew up loudly. Grasping the lid of the suitcase, I slowly lifted it open. The suitcase was nearly full with photos, cards, documents, and letters from years before.

In some ways, it was like Christmas, full of gifts of insight into loved ones that were captured in time. As I absently sifted through the documents, I noticed a creased corner of what looked to be a notecard of some sort, sticking out from beneath some yellowed newspaper clippings about World War II. I reached in carefully and grasped the bent corner. It was a postcard, complete with two one-cent postage stamps still affixed.

The precious postcard was faded, a red and blue illustration on the front. It had been written in pencil by my Norwegian grandfather from the beaches at Normandy to my grandmother in Illinois. He didn't write much; just a few lines assuring her he was okay, he missed her, and sending his love to her and their children (which included my dad). It was signed, "Love, Nels."

At first I thought how lovely it was that he took the time while in the midst of war to assure my grandmother he was okay. I can't imagine what it must have been like to be overseas at war in those days, far from your family, without the advent or benefit of computers, texting, FaceTime, or Skype.

But then, a smile slowly spread across my face. I felt as if my Grandpa had not only written the postcard to my Grandma, but also to me. His message came through, loud and clear. I finally had the answer to the question that had been plaguing my mind: I knew how I could contribute, how I could help; how I could make a difference.

I could write.

That was the "ah-ha" moment. I could write. Having an appreciation of what my grandfather's postcard must have meant to my grandmother, I figured that there had to be someone serving who would feel better by having a pen pal, a connection to the world outside of a war zone. The next question was, how to find that person.

Like so many times in my life when God has stepped in, the answer came swiftly and easily.

Fate intervenes

It was August 2004, and time for the 79th Annual Ioerger Family Reunion, in Metamora, IL, near my mom's hometown of Minonk. We had made the trek back to Illinois every year for the occasion, and this year, Mom and I were headed east yet again. I looked forward to seeing my grandma, along with the many aunts, uncles, and cousins who would be in attendance. Traditionally, close to 100 relatives from Mom's side of the family would gather for the daylong event that ended with a potluck dinner.

I was happy to spot my distant cousin, Karen, shortly after arriving, and we stood chatting, catching up on all that had happened since last year's reunion.

Karen had no sooner told me that her 19-year old daughter, Amy, was seriously dating a young man, then Amy came over and give me a big hug. Her eyes were shining as she told me about her boyfriend, Adam Schertz. Adam was serving in Iraq with his cousin, Jesse Schertz, and a friend, Tyler Ziegel. All three young men were from the surrounding area in Illinois. They were U.S. Marine Corp Reservists with Peoria County-based Company C, 6th Engineer Support Battalion.

I was excited to learn of Adam, Jesse, and Tyler, convinced that they were the Marines I was supposed to support. God surely sent these three brave young men to me to help. I asked Karen to get their addresses for me, which she did (thank you, Karen!). After getting back to Mission Viejo the end of August, I began writing and sending packages to all three Marines, to let them know that their service and sacrifice for our nation were appreciated.

Tyler and Adam were deep in the fight when we first began writing. Jesse was assigned to construction projects, so we had more time to talk; he and I spoke over AOL Messenger when we could. Jesse frequently talked about life in the Sandbox—Iraq—as well as his deep faith, and often quoted the Bible in our conversations. For a 19-year old young man, he was very insightful. Tyler and Adam would also write when they could, sharing their thoughts and feelings about being in Iraq, wanting to know how things were back home, maintaining a connection to the U.S. when they all were so far away.

For the next four months, I did all I could to provide comfort from home to "my three," as they affectionately became called. Adam's dad, Rod, even had a set of "civilian dog tags" made for me with a photo of each of the young men. I wore the three dog tags wherever I went, which invited a lot of questions from friends, members of my church, and even strangers.

Soon, others started sending cards; letters; and packages filled with everything from Gatorade drinks to beef jerky, Silly String to pillows, to the guys and their fellow Marines.

8

The power of the pen

The morning of Wednesday, December 22, 2004, dawned like any other day. I hopped on AOL Messenger at the normal time to talk with Jesse, but he didn't come online. It didn't strike me as odd, so I went about my day, my thoughts shifting to getting everything done in time for Christmas, just three days away.

Meanwhile, in the city of Fallujah, some 44 miles west of Baghdad, Tyler and Jesse were riding along with four other Marines in one of five trucks, returning to base. Suddenly, a loud explosion rang out. Al Qaeda had successfully sent a suicide bomber to take them out. The truck was totally decimated.

The phone rang and I picked it up.

"Suicide bomber got to a truck with Ty and Jesse. Ty is badly hurt, flown to Germany. Looks like Jesse didn't make it."

Honestly, I don't even remember who called—I was just in shock. I couldn't believe it. I didn't know what to do. I had never met Ty or Jesse, but I knew them. And just like that, in one instant, in one "wrong place/wrong time" moment, Jesse was gone, and Tyler's life would never be the same.

I don't really know how long I sat there, trying to make sense out of something so senseless. I could only imagine how bad Ty's injuries were if they had already sent him to Germany for medical attention. But the fact he had survived a suicide bomber attack was miraculous. I focused on that.

But Jesse. My heart ached for his loss, for his family and friends. I couldn't begin to comprehend how they must be feeling, especially three days before Christmas. I sat there thinking about our friendship and the tears came, but I didn't know how to handle it. Jesse and I had gotten to know one another well through writing and messengering for months, but there was no place for me to share my grief, no way to process this devastating news. We didn't share family or friends. It wasn't like when my dad had passed away, when the pain was eased as we all laughed and cried telling stories about his life. It was like stopping mid-sentence and never getting to finish what you had wanted to say.

> *But Jesse. My heart ached for his loss,*
> *for his family and friends.*

I tried to think of the best way to pay my respects to Jesse's family, to let them know I was so very sorry for their loss. I went to the store and tried to buy a sympathy card, but couldn't find one that fit the situation. Then I thought about the letters Jesse and I had written back and forth. I felt it might be of some comfort for his family to have those letters, to know his thoughts and feelings during the time before the suicide bomber had taken their son. I collected everything I had from Jesse and put it in a box and sent it along with a thank you card for the family's dedication.

Weeks went by, and I didn't hear back from Jesse's family. My brain rambled with an unrelenting internal dialogue. While I was sure (understandably) that they were enmeshed in their grief, I was a bit concerned they had not acknowledged my package. Maybe they hadn't gotten it. Maybe it wasn't the right thing to do after all, or it wasn't the right timing. I worried I had made things worse instead of better. I didn't know if they had known we were pen pals before I contacted them. And whether they did or didn't know before, they knew once they got my package; so, at that point, I didn't know how they felt about their 20-year old son having a 37-year old woman as a pen pal, even if it was totally innocent. They didn't know me! Maybe they had misunderstood my motivation, which really was only to be a patriotic American and to actively show support for our troops in action, to help. Simply put, I didn't know anything.

In mid-January 2005, I was in my home office planning an upcoming event, trying to put my focus on the myriad of details that are part of the job. The phone rang, and I answered it absently. I heard an unfamiliar woman's voice.

"Annie, this is Paula Schertz, Jesse's mom," she said. Before she could say another word, I whooped and started talking very fast.

"Hi, Paula! So nice to hear from you! It's so wonderful to hear your voice! I know we haven't met, but it's such a pleasure to speak with you!" I gushed, acting like a total dork. Paula interrupted me, her voice was stern and to the point.

"I'm here in San Antonio at Brooke Medical Center. Jesse survived, but he's burnt over 80 percent of his body and is facing double amputation"" — I couldn't believe what I was hearing!!! — and he's asking for his pen pal. Will you come?" she said.

"WHAT?! Jesse's ALIVE???" I tried not to scream in her ear.

"He is," she said, a bit confused, "badly hurt, but he made it. Forgive me, but I need to get back to Jesse. Someone will be in touch to arrange getting you to San Antonio in time for the surgery, if you'll come."

"Of course, I'll come," I said, elated. "Anything. Anything at all. Just let me know." And with that, we hung up.

I have no problem whatsoever telling you that after getting off the phone, I jumped up and down, screamed and whooped, and danced around my office before grabbing the phone and calling Mom, so glad to have a happy reason to call her. Pumpkin, still my constant companion, ran joyfully around the room with me.

"JESSE'S ALIVE! JESSE'S ALIVE!" I yelled, pacing back and forth in front of my desk as I told Mom about Paula's phone call. It was incredible! A miracle!

Later, I would learn from Jesse that after the explosion, Jesse had been thrown from the truck and had appeared to be dead. Somehow, as sometimes happens in the midst of chaos on the field following an attack, that had been communicated "down the line" in Iraq. But when the medics came to him and started to remove his dog tags to place on his toe for identification, Jesse had reached up and grabbed one of the medic's arms, saying, "I'm not dead! God saved me!"

When I had written to Jesse's parents, because I never mentioned anything about him dying, they thought the "difficult time" to which I referred was his sustaining severe injuries in the bomb blast. It was one big miscommunication, with the best possible outcome: Jesse was still alive.

A few weeks after getting the good news, Mom and I went to Illinois to visit my grandma. My grandma was doing great, and it was always so wonderful to see her. After settling in, my grandmother was filling us in on the family news. We were happy to learn that Adam was home on leave from Iraq. Adam and I were finally going to meet! Shortly after arriving, I headed over to cousin Karen's house. Adam told us that Jesse had come home for a family visit before having his amputation surgery. We thought it would be fun to surprise him, so Adam, Amy, my mom and I jumped in the car and headed straight over to Jesse's.

We drove up in front of the house and walked single file toward the front door, trying not to be too noisy so we didn't give away the surprise. Adam went through his aunt and uncle's door first, and I walked behind him. Adam suddenly stepped away, laughing, and Jesse looked up to see me standing there.

"Hey, Annie! What are you doing here?" he said, grinning broadly.

Just at that moment, Paula came into the den. There were hugs and tears all around, as everyone finally met, talking excitedly. We spent the better part of the day together, and after assuring Jesse I would come to San Antonio for his surgery, we left.

I couldn't help but smile as I drove back to my grandma's home. I couldn't put my finger on what was coming, exactly, but I knew in my heart that my life was about to change in a new direction. Dramatically. And boy, was I right!

9

An idea takes hold

As promised, a few weeks later I was flown, courtesy of a Marine family support group, to Brooke Army Medical Center in San Antonio, Texas. After deplaning and heading down the escalator toward baggage claim, I saw a soldier in uniform holding a sign with my name on it, who had been dispatched to drive me to the hospital.

An involuntary shudder went through me. I thought to myself a little fearfully, "I'm in *so* far over my head." I had never been to a military hospital, and I had no idea what I was doing. Most of all, I didn't want to do anything wrong, mindful that there were many military protocols of which I knew absolutely nothing. But at that point, all I could do was take things one step at a time, so I took a deep breath and smiled as the soldier and I walked to the waiting military car.

Arrangements had been made for me to stay at Fort Sam Houston's Fisher House, one of many "home away from home" housing facilities attached to military bases across the U.S. that provide complimentary housing for the families and military members receiving medical treatment. After being dropped off in the parking lot, I walked toward Fisher House's front door and saw a woman standing on the porch. We exchanged polite pleasantries, and introduced ourselves to each other, as you normally do in such situations. When she told me her name, I was stunned. She was Ty's mom! Ty was also at Brooke Medical Center! It was the most perfect serendipity I could have imagined.

I talked with Ty's mom on the porch and learned the extent of his injuries from the blast. They were traumatic, and his recovery was going to be a long one. The bomb had had some kind of chemical component which had caused third degree burns over much of his body, including significant burns on his face and head, as well as his right hand and left arm. He also had severe burns and trauma to his skull. Ultimately, Ty would lose his left arm and would have more than 30 surgeries to treat his injuries.

After talking to Becky for awhile, she gestured toward the door with a slight incline of her head. "Why don't you go see him now? I think it would be a great surprise, really make him happy," she said smiling, telling me how to find his room.

My heart was pounding as I walked down the hallway. Ty was the last of "my three" that I had yet to meet. I knocked on the door softly and stepped back a few steps as he quickly came to the door. As soon as he opened the door and caught sight of me, his face lit up, and he let out a big whoop. I burst into tears. We hugged, we cried; it was truly a joyous moment. I couldn't help but laugh, too. Ty had on a helmet with a small license plate on the back that said, "Tyler," and he was wearing a shirt that said, "Your girlfriend wants me." Such an amazing attitude! And a great sense of humor, especially under the circumstances.

After visiting with Ty, I found Jesse and his family; his surgery had gone well. Jesse seemed upbeat and I soon learned why: the news was better than expected! The doctors had managed to save his right leg; the left leg was amputated below the knee. Thankfully, Jesse came through the surgery without any other complications.

After three days, I left San Antonio and headed back home to California, amid promises to stay in touch, and to come back to visit. It was hard to say good-bye to Jesse and Ty, as well as their families. Seeing the many, many young men at Brooke (at that point, women weren't serving on the battlefield, so the patients were men) fueled my desire to do more. Surely if people knew what these brave men were going through, they would help and support them.

The seeds were planted. And, as often happens in God's plan for your life, I may not have realized it at that moment; but the seeds *were* planted.

The question that haunted me

I made several trips back to Brooke Medical Center. Each time I went, Jesse would tell the other patients that I was "from Hollywood," even though I corrected him and said no, I was simply from Orange County. But to Jesse, since I was from Southern California, that equated to the entertainment industry.

Remember, back in 2005 all our wounded heroes had in their hospital rooms was a TV. There was no social media, smart phones, or tablets to connect them to their loved ones and world. Their media resources in the hospital were minimal. So, when I would be in the room, Jesse or one of the other patients would grab their remotes and ask me, "*Does America support us?*" because they were not seeing that on the TV.

Not wanting to add any more pain to those who already had suffered so much, I deflected the question, unwilling to bring the controversy and societal debate about the wars into the veterans' lives. It was better that they remained somewhat insulated while recovering, the pain of the growing disconnect between those who served and those who didn't would be apparent soon enough when they went home.

"Does America support us?"

That said, their question rang in my head often. I had had no idea what the military world was, had had absolutely zero connection with anyone in the military, and suddenly I was being given opportunities to be a part of that world as a civilian. Chance encounters—if you believe in them—with military personnel kept happening, and opportunities to become more involved with the military literally fell into my lap. It truly was God in action.

I suddenly realized that I needed to help others "get" it, too.

Just a God thing

After one of my trips to San Antonio, I flew home to California and met with a dear friend and entertainment attorney, Frank Wheaton. I'll never forget the conversation.

"Frank, I know what I'm supposed to do," I said determinedly over dinner. Frank wrinkled his brow and smiled, because he knows me very well—and he knows that when I get an idea in my head, there's no talking me out of it.

"What do you mean, Annie?" he asked patiently, still smiling.

"We're going to create a non-profit organization that honors, supports, celebrates, and thanks our nation's veterans; and we're going to take the politics out of supporting our veterans; and we're going to create television shows that honor, support, and celebrate veterans; and we're going to change the medium; and we're going to change television; because no matter how bad the economy gets, everyone will always have a TV, and TV has never done right by our veterans," I said rapidly without taking a breath.

Frank had been listening intently and respectfully while I had run the race of my ideas, and he started to chuckle when I finished. "Is that all, Annie?" he asked, before we both burst out loud laughing.

"That said and all kidding aside," Frank continued in a more serious tone, "you know it's not going to be easy. That is not an easy sell in Hollywood, and despite your most sincere efforts, which I both see and appreciate, it will be hard to keep this from being political. They're going to make it political. They're going to put your show in a 'red' bucket, they're going to paint *you* red, and that's where it will stay. What you want to have happen, probably won't happen."

"Why? I don't understand that," I said angrily, not at him, but at the thought, "taking care of our veterans and saying 'thank you' shouldn't matter whether you vote red or blue or purple! Supporting our veterans and saying thank you and doing it right isn't political! It doesn't have to be, and it never should be!"

"I can't disagree, Annie. I'll stand behind you, I'll help you, and I'll do whatever you want me to do. But just know from the outset that it's going to be a very hard thing to accomplish," he said smiling and nodding his head gently, because that is how Frank is: Sincere, genuine, and always willing to help.

> *"Supporting our veterans and saying thank you and doing it right isn't political!"*

"Thank you, Frank. I hear you. But you know what I believe: With the faith of the proverbial mustard seed, you can tell that mountain to move," I said in reply, smiling, "and it's time for me to take that mustard seed. It's simple; it's just a 'God thing.'"

It really *was* that simple, to me. This idea was a culmination of my background in journalism and television, combined with my desire to make a difference for vets outside of politics. Having witnessed the critical needs of our veterans firsthand, I wanted to take their message to the public. The more I learned about the unspeakable sacrifices made by our nation's heroes and the problems they were facing coming home, the more I knew that I had to do this. I firmly believed that if Americans knew of the veterans' plight, they would do something about it.

We moved forward quickly. Frank's honest counsel and accurate assessment of the industry that night was not an indication of a lack of support for me or for what I wanted to do; his actions showed quite the contrary. Soon after our business dinner, he set about taking care of the legalities of creating "The American Soldier Network," to accomplish the goals I had outlined to Frank.

Another piece to this life-puzzle — or, more to the point, life-solution — for me was the blessing of my prior physical trauma. I say "blessing" because the experiences I had gone through physically provided me with the opportunity to have relatability with veterans who had hidden wounds.

To be clear, I don't mean in any way at all to equate what I went through with the trauma of war; but I had been an advocate of compassion for those with invisible wounds for years, since I knew what it felt like for people to not understand the very real, very physical and emotional impact of post-traumatic stress and injuries that were not obvious. Now, that pain was put to good use — a silver lining that would soon be a salve on my own personal wounds.

PILLAR #3

Create a personal mission statement.

" And we know that in all things God works for the good of those who love him, who have been called according to his purpose."

Romans 8:28-30

PILLAR #3

Create a personal mission statement.

" And we know that in all things God works for the good of those who love him, who have been called according to his purpose."

Romans 8:28-30

Pillar #3: Create a personal mission statement.

A mission statement helps you find your focus. And focus is critical when you're coming back from a crisis.

A mission statement can be your touchstone, something you can cling to and look to for inspiration and guidance.

Big businesses pay big bucks for consultants to come in and create mission statements for them, because their CEOs and boards understand the power of mission.

You can create your personal mission statement much more easily than that.

When I was in college, I read the book *The Path: Creating Your Mission Statement for Work and for Life* by Laurie Beth Jones. Through a series of exercises and step-by-step guidance, the book challenges you to define your personal mission statement in two words.

My personal mission statement became "Ignite faith." I've gone back a couple of times to re-read the book, thinking that my mission statement must have evolved over time or I could fine tune it. But, nope. "Ignite faith" it is and will ever be. It works for me.

Everyone will take something different from *The Path* and that's the point: a personal mission statement is *personal*. I really encourage you to take some time here and develop a true personal mission statement and set out to live by it.

Once you've finishing reading this book, go and get *The Path*. It's on Amazon for less than the cost of a movie ticket. (And I don't make any commission from referring the book, either.)

Missions & the military

I want to tell a quick story specifically for any military service members or military veterans reading this. Creating a personal mission statement is even more critical for you. Here's why: when you're on active duty, everything is mission-centric, right? Everything you do is about the mission.

It can be no different when you're back in civilian life. When you come home, civilian life is way less structured — and lots of veterans struggle. But you can still live a mission-centered life. Only it's *your* mission, not the one set out by your CO.

I once met a Special Forces guy who wasn't feeling as significant out of the military as he was in the military. He was used to high-stress, intense situations and life was boring by comparison. He was, in technical terms, in a funk.

I talked with him about creating a personal mission statement, and it completely shifted his perspective about civilian life. He became more focused and driven and got out of his funk. Having a mission again changed his life and his business.

If you're a veteran and you're struggling to find your focus as a civilian, I encourage you to read and work through *The Path*. And, if you need more support, please check out the Resources page at the end of this book for more ideas and organizations that can help.

10

We interrupt this program

In November 2008, I went to a friend's birthday party at bar in Arizona called the Salty Senorita. Part of the charm of this place is a conversation swing in the courtyard where you can sit and hang out while you wait for a table.

There I was, sitting in the swing and chatting with a friend, when suddenly someone pushed me from behind. I wasn't expecting it and I flipped out of the swing and hit my head. A softball-sized lump immediately swelled up on the back of my head, but I toughed it out and got some ice from the restaurant. In truth, I was seeing stars and only found out the next day that I had a concussion.

My doctor prescribed me Soma for the headaches I was experiencing. I had a brain scan that was declared "all clear." Still, the headaches got worse as the months went by. I had ringing in my ears and saw an ear doctor. I felt tingling in my face and saw a dermatologist. Every few weeks the headaches would be so bad I would go to the ER, where they would treat me for dehydration and send me home.

I had another massive headache attack in 2010 when my mom happened to be visiting me. I was throwing up non-stop (a usual symptom of one of these attacks) and my mom was a little freaked out.

I was convulsing by the time we reached the ER, where I was given the standard hydration treatment three times with no relief. Finally, the ER doctor agreed to a brain scan, although he said, "We're not going to find anything."

They wheeled me in and out of the CT scanning room in a matter of minutes. A short time later, the ER doctor came into my room and flopped down on the end of my bed.

"You have a massive tumor in the middle of your head," he said.

My thoughts raced, and I wanted to break down, but I had to keep it together with my mom in the room. The hospital staff quickly raced me down the hallway for an MRI scan.

The tumor in my head was a whopping 6.5 cm—about 2.5 inches. In other words, not small as brain tumors go. The doctor wanted to do surgery the next day.

I was moved to a room in the Intensive Care Unit. When I looked up, there was a stained-glass panel on the ceiling depicting clouds and blue sky. I mean, who designed this? If you're in the ICU and you already think you're dying, the last thing you want is a reminder of heaven!

I called my pastor who came to offer me spiritual support and guidance. I decided I wanted a second opinion, rather than rushing into surgery. After all, I'd been dealing with this for two years, what was another day? I called my pro athlete friends for their recommendations for a neurologist. The same name kept coming up: Dr. Steven Giannotta, chair of the neurological surgery department at the University of Southern California.

The next morning when the neurosurgeon brought in the surgery release form, I said I wanted a second opinion. The surgeon said I was too risky to move, but he asked who I wanted to see. (In my experience, doctors don't take it well when you want a second opinion.) I said Dr Steven Giannotta at USC.

The surgeon said, "Well he is the best there is. *If* you can get in to him I will authorize it."

I said, "He is waiting."

Lucky for me, Dr. Giannotta agreed to review my case, so my mom drove me over to USC to await his opinion. I swear when he walked into the room, he had such an air of confidence, all I could hear in my head was the theme from *Top Gun*.

"That's one hell of a golf ball you've got in your head," he said as he tossed the CD with my scans onto the desk. He agreed to do the surgery but said I'd have to wait at least ten days as he was going on vacation with his family.

I figured, sure, why not? I was in no rush to have my head cut open.

In the meantime, he gave me a drug called Decadron to shrink the swelling in my brain before surgery. While the swelling may have shrunk, I certainly didn't! I ballooned 35 pounds in three weeks.

> *"That's one hell of a golf ball you've got in your head."*

The day before my scheduled surgery, the doctor's office called and said that my insurance company wouldn't cover the surgery; they deemed it "elective." (Really? Thanks, Obamacare!) The doctor's office advised me to go to the ER and come in that way, and that's what we did.

What was supposed to be a four-hour surgery took ten hours and 45 minutes. But it was a success! The tumor was gone. Unfortunately, so was the hearing in my right ear.

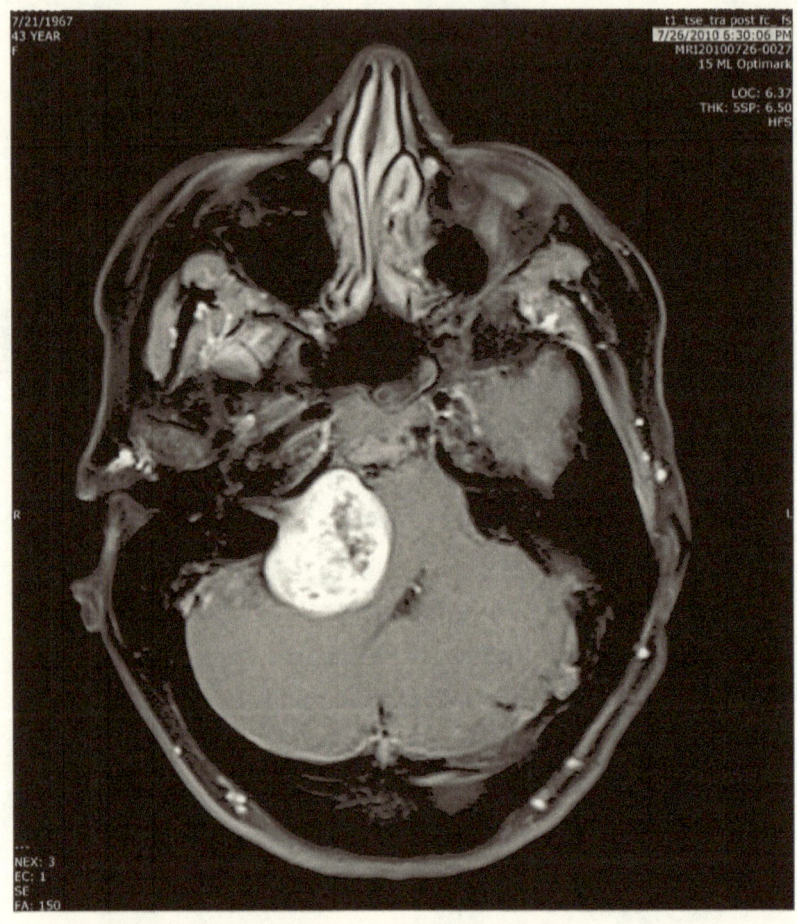

Thankfully the tumor wasn't cancerous, but it was deemed an acoustic neuroma, a benign tumor that grows on the balance and hearing nerves that lead from the inner ear to your brain.

When you lose your hearing, you lose your balance. When you have no balance, your ability to walk, or even stand up, is affected. I couldn't walk, and while my brain kept searching for equilibrium, I was projectile vomiting on the regular.

The challenge of my life

And then there was my face. My overall look was that of a half-blinking, half-smiling sumo wrestler. I had staples down one side of my head. And remember, I'd gained weight before the surgery and then the post-surgical swelling added to my glamorous look. I'm surprised the orderlies weren't lining up to date me!

The hardest part was seeing the look of abject pity on people's faces when they came to visit me.

After my surgery my face was so distorted it looked like my face slid considerably south, almost like I'd had a stroke. Luckily, a neurologist friend had told me to chew 2 pieces of Bazooka bubble gum as soon as I was out of surgery — and for weeks afterward. Chewing the gum was exercise for my facial muscles. Sure enough, within a few weeks my face was looking mostly back to normal. I chewed so much gum that to this day I can't stand the smell of bubble gum!

I was determined to walk as soon as possible. My medical team challenged me to walk twice around the nurses' station before I could go home. The recommended in-hospital recovery was ten to 14 days, but I fought to get out in only four days. Looking back, that wasn't a great decision on my part — but have I mentioned, I'm stubborn?

Once home, I had to keep my head at a perfect 90-degree angle or hello, massive waves of nausea! I slept sitting straight up in a chaise lounge I had brought in from the patio.

The aftermath of my surgery was probably my biggest test of faith in my life. I knew the journey ahead would be harder than my recovery after the assault. This was my *brain*. I had to learn how to speak again. I needed physical therapy to learn how to walk again, not only because of the loss of balance but also because my body was so weak. It took two years of constant exercises and determined work I get back to a normal walking gait.

And while I'm still in physical therapy, I can now go to the gym a few times a week.

The aftermath of my surgery was probably my biggest test of faith in my life.

There are still times that I will turn my head too quickly, or get up from bed at just the right angle to have a flare up of imbalance and disorientation. And, I have constant ringing in my right ear that sounds like a high-pitched drill.

Am I tempted to feel sorry for myself? At times, you bet. But then, I come back to my mission. The truth is, I needed American Soldier Network as much as it needed me. Fighting for our active duty and veteran servicemembers gives me a reason to get out of bed every morning and come out swinging for the rafters.

11

The idea takes off

When I had the idea to serve the veteran community, I legally converted Angels Within—the non-profit I had started in 1996—to an all-veteran and military charity. We changed the focus and mission of the organization, and updated our IRS filing to reflect our new military focus.

Learning as we grow

There's so much I would do differently if I created American Soldier Network (ASN) today. In the beginning, I didn't know what I didn't know. For example, not every servicemember is a "soldier"—that's an Army term—although we serve veterans of all branches. I thought I was being inspired; after all, I got the name from a Toby Keith song!

I wanted to raise awareness to the needs of both veterans and active-duty military servicemembers here at home. I called it a network because a network makes connections. It connects the dots.

Getting ASN off the ground was an uphill climb. We had little to no funding. Our staff is purely volunteer and I still do all the marketing and PR myself. I was lucky to have my mom's financial support, because any money I raised went to programming, and not in my pocket.

There came a point that I thought about getting a "real" job; running a non-profit is humbling. Making no salary is a hit to the ego. You have to set your ego and your pride aside when you're obeying your calling and doing something for the greater good.

Because of my entertainment background, I've been able to ask celebrities to lend their name to the cause. Celebrities are constantly asked for money for great causes — and they can't give to all of them. They're asked to attend dozens of events for great causes — and they can't attend them all. I understand that, and I think that's what has made my celebrity outreach so successful.

You have to set your ego and your pride aside when you're obeying your calling and doing something for the greater good.

We started to gain momentum and things progressed organically. One key that helped was staying true to the vision but flexible in the execution.

I originally envisioned a TV show with a pro-veteran slant. But what took off was a Stockings for Soldiers project for injured active-duty servicemembers at Camp Pendleton near San Diego. With no budget, we grew this program with in-kind donations from our sponsors like Warner Bros. and Snap-On Tools. Every year we take swag bags full of gifts to hundreds of servicemembers.

We're now in our 15th year of this incredible outreach program, and we've expanded to Hearts for Heroes, which replicates the swag bag idea for Valentine's Day. We're showing our wounded warriors that America is grateful for their service.

What people don't see is the red tape we have to get through every year. Each bag has to be identical. We have to have the gifts approved by the government ahead of time. We need authorization to access the base and hand out the bags. There are so many rules that I had no idea when I started down this path. I'm lucky that everyone has been great to work with as I figured things out. At times I felt like a blind person finding my way with a stick. Now I know what questions to ask when we want to implement a new program.

ASN has evolved as I've identified or distilled down to the core needs of our veterans. One of my favorite programs to do is our Junior Patriots presentation at school assemblies. We talk about what it means to serve, and I would bring Eddie and Hazel along and talk about how they serve. Then the kids get to give back to veterans and servicemembers as they make handmade cards that go inside the Christmas and Valentine swag bags.

When we expanded our service programs into suicide prevention, we partnered with an organization that provides shoes in Third World countries. We collect shoes—and our supporters collect shoes all over the country—and we're paid 40 cents for every pound of shoes. It's a win-win; they get shoes to help shoe the world, and we get funding for our programs. Check out the Resources page at the end of this book to learn more about ASN's programs and how you can help!

Starting a non-profit: a word of warning

Let me offer a bit of advice to anyone who has thought, "I want to do good. I think I'll start a non-profit." In a word, don't.

Don't do it. Instead, consider starting a for-profit company that donates its proceeds to a non-profit.

Here's why: there are thousands of non-profits competing for dollars. The competition is extreme. In the veteran space alone, there are 45,000 non-profit organizations. And, chances are, no matter how unique or compelling you think your idea is, there's probably a non-profit already out there doing what you want to do.

And then there's the red tape. In the U.S., the Internal Revenue Service's tax code governs the tax treatment of non-profits. Trust me when I say there are a lot of hoops to jump through to obtain the coveted 501(c)(3) status that makes you a non-profit.

Then each state has different non-profit laws, so if you have donors from multiple states, you have to comply with each state's law.

The only real benefit to the donor is the charitable donation tax deduction — and those tax laws are tightening up, too.

The non-profit doesn't pay federal income taxes, but if you have employees you still have to comply with all the state laws and various taxes like employment taxes. And you have to make sure you don't make too much unrelated business income, or there's tax consequences.

> *The only real benefit to the donor is the charitable donation tax deduction.*

See what a morass this is? And I'm just scratching the surface. If I'd have known then what I know now, I wouldn't have started a non-profit. I would have found a different way to serve the veterans we serve at American Soldier Network.

Doing good for others is an amazing feeling. If you see a need in your community and you feel compelled to do something about it — yay! We need more people like you.

My advice is, do the research and find a non-profit who's already addressing that need or is working in that space. Start with your local community foundation and see how you can contribute to an existing charity or help them expand their services. Or, maybe you can start a local chapter of a national non-profit.

There's really no need to reinvent the wheel. Rather, be a spoke in someone else's wheel. Provide momentum to a wheel that's already rolling. Partner up. Smaller non-profits need help, not more competition.

> *My advice is, do the research and find a non-profit who's already addressing that need or is working in that space.*

Plus, you might find that the real need isn't what you thought when you had your idea for a non-profit. One thing I learned in working with veterans with PTS and TBI, and studying veteran suicide rates, is that there is no single cause, and no single cure. Everyone will heal differently. What works for one vet, might not work for another.

That's why it's so disappointing to see the competition among non-profits who serve veterans but try to shout the loudest "we're the best solution, support us" — it shuts off any sense of collaboration or uniting resources to address real veterans' real needs.

If you're determined to start a non-profit, find out what the real need is — not what you think it is, or what fun bandage you want to put on it. In the veteran space, for example, there are non-profits that take veterans hiking, or to baseball games, or to Disneyland, all in the name of treating PTS. Those are all great ideas — but is that what veterans *need* to address their core issues or actually heal their brains?

As jaded as all of that sounds, it also motivates me to be a force for radical, life-saving change.

PILLAR #4

Assemble your team.

"For the body is not one member, but many."

1 Corinthians 12:14

Pillar #4: Assemble your team.

No one does anything alone; we all need other people. Even if you think you don't need anyone, remember this: did you milk the cow to put cream in your coffee this morning? Did you grow the wheat to make your bagel? Probably not.

We all rely on and need other people in a thousand ways every day.

When you're coming back from a crisis, it's important to figure out who will help you rebound and succeed. Reach out and create your support system for your physical healing, day-to-day life (like rides to medical appointments) and spiritual and emotional needs.

Your team does not need to be around you every day. Your team can be made up of medical professionals, friends and family, your pastor, local delivery services, and even your pets (more on that later).

For me, I had a small circle of life-long girlfriends to lean on during my crisis times. My parents were there for me as well, especially during my recovery after the assault.

But the biggest team I have is my medical team, some of whom, like my physical therapists Joe and Laura, have been with me for more than 20 years now through all the ups and downs.

I feel so blessed to have a core medical team that can reach out and bring in specialists when needed, who know my complete medical history and what works and doesn't work for me.

My pain management team led by Dr. Lowenstein has been a constant in my life since the airplane assault. It's not like seeing a doctor once every few years when you get the flu. These people know me inside and out (literally). The location of the pain may have changed—from my back after the assault to the near-constant headaches with my brain tumors—but their care has never wavered.

I'm eternally grateful to each and every one of them!

Eddie & Hazel

Growing up, dogs were always a part of our daily life—somewhere there's a picture of a puppy in my crib! My canine companions have been a big part of my story and how I've gotten through my life challenges. After all, "God" spelled backwards is "dog." I believe they are truly one of God's greatest gifts to us humans, for us to experience true unconditional love and loyalty.

In 1994 I got my first Rhodesian Ridgeback and named her Pumpkin. She was an amazing dog! I didn't know it at the time, but Ridgebacks are the number one companion for children with autism. They have a keen sense of empathy and somehow know when someone is in pain.

It might seem odd to include pets in your crisis recovery team, but without Pumpkin, I know I wouldn't have gotten through the airline assault, much less losing my dad.

After Pumpkin, I got Eddie and Hazel—brother and sister from a litter born the same day Pumpkin died: July 25, 2008.

Eddie and Hazel were by my side for the brunt of the ickyness before and after my brain tumor surgeries. Eddie in particular was so in tune with my physical being. I would be

on the floor of my bathroom, puking my guts out, and there was Eddie laying right next to me. He instinctively knew when I needed him; he'd rest his head on my leg or put a paw on me like a protective field of dog love.

I was devastated when Eddie passed away in January 2019, and Hazel was a bit lost as well. Now Hazel sticks to me like glue and follows me everywhere; she's definitely taken over Eddie's role

Particularly for people who live alone, dogs are like little fur angels. If you're going through a tough time emotionally or physically, dogs let you know you're not alone. It's somehow reassuring to know that another being knows you're in pain. They just love on you. And those days that you don't feel like getting out of bed, they give you a reason to. They get you outside and walking so you're not stagnant. They give you something besides yourself to focus on, when all you want to do is curl up into a ball and cry.

Now, if you're coming out of a crisis situation and you've never had dogs, I'm not suggesting that you go and get a dog right now. That could be very stressful for both of you! However, there are other ways to experience the joy and love of a fur angel. Volunteer at a local animal shelter. Ask a friend with a dog to spend some time with their pup. Check with home-health agencies for a canine comfort program.

Then, when you're ready, take the leap and get a dog (or a cat) to be your constant companion.

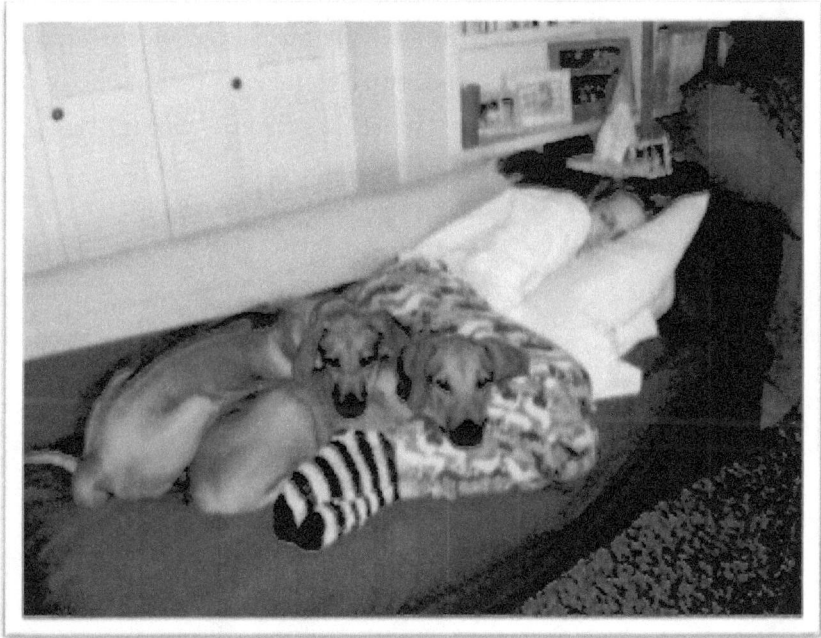

A note about no-shows

Often throughout life, people tell you to your face they will help you, and offer all kinds of promises. And then ... nothing. They don't follow through. They don't deliver.

I've had this happen so many times, more so with volunteers or "supporters" of my non-profit than with my health, thank goodness. It's so easy to let this get under your skin, to feel frustrated and hurt when someone doesn't follow through on their promises.

Remember, no one hurts you unless you let them. Find a way to move on, let the negative, sad, let-down feelings go and push on.

On the flip side, be accountable! If you say you will do something, show up, keep your word and lead by example. Be resilient despite the outside let downs.

I've had more people offer me promises that were empty. Sure, it hurt and was a hill to climb, but once I learned who was truly there for me and my work—and who was not—the growth was immeasurable.

12

Rewriting the suicide story

As I dug deeper into the needs of our veterans returning home and re-integrating into civilian life, I was struck by the reality of veteran suicide. Since I'm a journalist at heart, I wanted to know as much as I could, so I could perhaps help in some way to prevent even one veteran from taking his or her life.

Learning the truth

Let me preface this section by saying that I am not an expert in suicide prevention. I have no background in medicine or psychology. But, for some reason known only to God, this is the path that was chosen for me. I agreed to go down this path because of everything I went through.

You've probably heard the statistic: 22 veterans commit suicide every day. When that number was released by the VA in its 2012 *Suicide Data Report*, the internet went wild. Every day brought a new social media meme or a push-up challenge. Non-profits popped up practically overnight, determined to prevent veteran suicide. The media fixated on that number, and so we did, too.

No one questioned it. But in fact, that number was never accurate. If anything, it's low. Last year the VA released a new report where it admitted that the 2012 study included active-duty suicides. One to four active-duty servicemembers take their own life every day. We lose more active duty servicemembers to suicide than to combat, but that is never reported.

The 2012 report analyzed death certificates from only 21 states between 1999 and 2011, and the accuracy of veteran identifiers on the certificates was speculative at best. For example, the average age for veteran suicide based on this study was about 60 years old — clearly not veterans of Iraq and Afghanistan.

> *We lose more active duty servicemembers to suicide than to combat.*

Moreover, the 29 states missing from this report, included California and Texas — two states with huge veteran populations. And, the VA reports only include documented deaths of veterans who were in the VA system. Thousands more never seek treatment through the VA.

Why now, but not then?

There's no one issue causing suicide and no one answer to prevent it — and that can feel frustrating. One thing I wondered about was the generational differences between returning WWII veterans and today's veterans.

Of the 14 million Americans who served in the military during WWII, nearly 500,000 are still alive. These veterans are living into their 80s and 90s. They weren't committing suicide when they came home. Why not? World War II was horrific by all accounts — even more so than the wars in Iraq and

Afghanistan. And, many post-9/11 veteran suicide victims didn't see combat. So, it's not just a "horror of war" or combat issue.

I discovered several key differences between WWII and post 9/11 veterans—mostly to do with the service itself.

In WWII, the average soldier was 26 years old. The draft, instituted by Congress in 1940, required men aged 18 to 45 to register. About 61 percent of WWII servicemembers were drafted; the other 39 percent volunteered.

Today, most new military recruits are enlisting at 18 or 19 years old. When you consider that most bipolar disorders and schizophrenia patients aren't diagnosed until their 20s, you will have a certain percentage of veterans who will have mental illness regardless of their service. This automatically puts them in a higher risk category for suicide.

Next, consider how troops were transported in WWII and today. Troops traveled by ship in the 1940's. So, it took weeks to get home from a deployment. That meant time with their buddies to decompress, and talk.

Today, troops return by plane, sometimes by themselves and not with their company, and they can be back with their families in a day. That sense of togetherness and camaraderie is stripped away almost instantly. Who can they talk to when they need to? A psychologist at a VA clinic? Make an appointment and they'll to get to you ... and then medicate you.

It's astonishing how many veterans I've talked to who are disenchanted with the VA's treatment of PTS. (And no one is even talking about the pre-cursor to PTS, post-traumatic growth.) Most veterans receive a "one-size-fits-all" diagnosis and a prescription for anti-psychotic medication—whether that's the answer or not. If the meds aren't helping, many quit cold-turkey (never a good idea—do not do this!) because they can't get an appointment to adjust their dosage or get a weaning schedule.

I'm not suggesting that everyone who returns home from deployment comes back broken. Far from it. And in fact, veteran suicide isn't always driven by PTS. It could be financial stress, childhood issues that come up, or even drug and alcohol abuse.

In addition, suicide isn't just a problem in the veteran community. It's an epidemic facing all of the America. Veteran statistics simply attract media attention. But in truth, suicide is the #2 killer of all 10- to 25-year-olds. And, the World Health Organization predicts depression will be the number one leading cause of disease burden globally by the year 2030.

> *I'm not suggesting that everyone who returns home from deployment comes back broken.*
> *Far from it.*

No matter what the circumstance, those who do need support sometimes have a hard time finding what they need.

In 2014, I attended the funerals of 30 veterans and nine active duty servicemembers, all of whom I had met through American Soldier Network. They had all committed suicide.

The father of one of the men came to me after the funeral and asked for help. His son had come home on leave and was supposed to return to duty. But, rather than return, he chose to end his life. His family, understandably, was devastated. Why their son? What had happened? Their son had never been diagnosed with depression or PTS, and exhibited no outward signs.

Then, when I read that veterans are literally killing themselves in the parking of a VA facility because they're so frustrated with the care (or lack of care) they're receiving, that was the final straw. I knew I had to do something. I thought, how can I re-create that sense of camaraderie, where veterans can talk and share and relate to one another in a way that no one else can?

Filling the void

I started RuckUp.org in January 2018 and envisioned it as the first site dedicated to stopping veteran suicide by putting veterans in touch with other veterans. Through a private chat area called "The Foxhole" veterans—who are ID verified—can chat online with their peers. I called it The Foxhole because it's meant to replicate that community and camaraderie that they experienced on active duty. A place they can talk freely and openly and without judgment. A place they can express themselves in a way they may not be able to with family or friends who don't have similar experiences.

Veterans who use RuckUp are also asked to sign the Choose to Live Oath. Military servicemembers resonate with an oath. When they're sworn into military service, they take an oath to serve the country and uphold the constitution. So, I thought, let's give them a new oath—an oath to live. Through the Aid Station we provide contact information for resources—not just VA resources—of practitioners and facilities that treat PTS, TBI and depression. There's also a Caregiver's Corner where caregivers can get support and information.

I CHOOSE TO LIVE

I do solemnly swear that I will support and defend the Constitution of the United States against all enemies, foreign and domestic.

I choose to appreciate each day.

I choose not to let my demons get the best of me.

I choose to buddy check those I can get in touch with.

I choose to reach out when I feel things are getting tough.

I choose to count my blessings NOT my battles.

I choose to believe I am worthy.

I choose to stay plugged in to those who support me.

I choose to be there for my brothers/sisters.

I choose to not abuse my body, substances and the like.

I choose to stay grounded in faith, family & brotherhood.

I choose to LIVE!

RuckUp.org is free to veterans and their families. (The Foxhole is veterans only, but anyone can access the other resources on the site.)

It took a lot of work and a lot of technical skills (not mine) to get RuckUp.org up and running. When I was meeting with the programmers at Surface 51, I was negotiating with them to donate some of their time. Our meeting was interrupted when one of the gentlemen got a call that a buddy of his had just committed suicide. The importance and urgency of this project ratcheted up considerably for them in that moment, and I'm extremely grateful for all of their efforts to make RuckUp.org a reality.

So far, just from feedback about the Oath, we've heard from 20 veterans who say that the Oath has given them a reason to choose to live. It's literally saving lives that would have been lost to suicide, and those are just the ones we heard from.

To say that the feedback has been positive is an understatement, and we're expanding our efforts to get the word out to all veterans about the site.

Rewriting the veteran story

Beyond the one-on-one support through RuckUp.org, I'm determined to change the way America thinks about mental health in general and veterans in particular.

If you're tagged as having "mental health" issues—for any reason, even if it's situational like a parent or spouse dying—there's a stigma to that. It's a cloud that follows you everywhere. It impacts how people see you, behave around you, or even talk to you. (Or avoid you.)

So, if you have a fear of losing your job or being passed up for promotion because of "mental health," are you more or less likely to ask for help addressing your PTS or depression?

What if we could change all of that and de-stigmatize mental health? What if people understood that PTS isn't a life sentence, that it can absolutely be overcome?

After my assault in 1994, long before my work with the veteran community, I became fascinated with the brain. It's a powerful tool and I'm living proof that the brain can be healed from trauma, if you do the work. Everyone has the ability to heal their brain!

I began referring to mental health as brain health. The brain is *physically* affected by "mental" issues — and the brain can be healed and new neuropathways created.

> *Everyone has the ability to heal their brain!*

Just like the 22 veteran statistic created a media storm, changing how we talk about and deal with brain health starts with the media. It's the media that can change the mindset of the masses.

That's why I created the *American Heroes* television show — to bring positive storylines and characters to mainstream media. The show focuses on veterans who continue to serve in some way — maybe they've overcome challenges and started a successful business or they support philanthropic causes.

With my connections to the media and entertainment industries, I'm always looking for ways to influence how the news and television shows portray veteran issues, to move away from gloom and doom and instead show more positives and the successes. It's a longer and more arduous task, but I'm convinced that it's the best way to change how we talk about veteran issues and release the stigma.

Until then, I write a monthly column with the same perspective as the TV show. A few years ago I started the "American Heroes" column for the *U.S. Veterans Magazine*. Each month I feature a veteran who is making a difference, showing what's possible when you can heal your issues and go on to serve in new ways. It's a true celebration of our veteran community.

I must be doing something right; ASN is receiving attention on a national level (like our NASCAR car!), and I'm stretching to new heights as well. At times it feels like a rollercoaster, and I'm going to keep on riding.

13

The highest high, and another blow

When I look back at so much of my life, it's almost shocking to see how time and again the past foreshadowed the future.

In college I joined the speech team on the recommendation of Dr. Buck. He encouraged me to compete in the impromptu and persuasive speaking categories. Impromptu speaking is where you're given a topic and you have five minutes to prepare a speech about it. Persuasive speaking is a prepared speech that's meant to move people to action.

Because of my acting background, speech competitions came easily to me and I had fun! I never had any stage fright, in fact I'm quite the opposite: the bigger the crowd the more confident I am. Little did I know how handy these skills would become later in life!

After my airline assault and working with a psychiatrist to overcome the symptoms of post-traumatic stress, people started asking me to come and share my story. Then they were fascinated by PTS: what it's like to be diagnosed, how I got through it, and why I'm adamant that it's neither a "syndrome" nor a "disorder."

In the beginning of my speaking career, I was asked to speak at churches and women's group, just to share my story.

As my life and work evolved, so did my speaking. When my pen pal story (as it's become known) unfolded, people wanted to hear about that. People would come up to me afterwards and say how inspired they were, how one idea and one act of kindness could start a movement. My presentations became inspirational talks and keynote speeches. And I was now getting paid to speak. How unreal is that?

My college impromptu speaking sure paid off! I've only written one speech, for a keynote presentation at a business organization. I spent three painful weeks researching numbers and statistics. It was awful—so outside my comfort zone!

But I practiced and prepared, and when I got to the event, the organizer said, no, we just want to hear your story! Thank goodness, I thought! I threw away my notes and never wrote another speech again. I also learned to clarify what the event organizer wants their audience to hear.

Reaching a pinnacle

Speaking engagements have come up by word of mouth and people hearing about my story, and wanting me to share it. In February 2018, shortly after launching RuckUp.org, I received an invitation to speak at the LIFTx event at MacDill Air Force Base in Florida. Think of a TED talk at a military base, and you've got the idea.

I was elated—and more than a little humbled.

Everyone on the base was in the audience that day, from the base commander on down the ranks. Air Force One was sitting on the tarmac. The president wasn't there, but top brass had flown in from Washington. This was a big deal.

DEPARTMENT OF THE AIR FORCE
6TH AIR MOBILITY WING (AMC)
MACDILL AIR FORCE BASE, FLORIDA

FEB 0 9 2018

Colonel April D. Vogel, USAF
Commander
6th Air Mobility Wing
8208 Hanger Loop Drive
MacDill AFB FL 33621

Dear Ms. Annie Nelson,

On behalf of the 19,000 men and women stationed at MacDill AFB, I would like to thank you for your willingness to come and speak to our Soldiers, Sailors, Marines, and Airmen at LIFTx 2018. You are part of an elite line-up of leaders and influencers and we thank you for your willingness to contribute your time and energy to this incredible effort!

Your heartfelt message delivered directly to service members, who serve globally, will help encourage, inspire, motivate, and enrich our members and leaders. We look forward to hearing your stories and insights.

As our guest, please let us know if there is anything we can do to make your visit more enjoyable. My Commanders Action Group, is standing by to support. Thank you again for supporting LIFTx!

Sincerely

APRIL D. VOGEL, Colonel, USAF

MISSION FOCUSED...VALUED AIRMEN

It was an awe-inspiring scene, and the biggest audience I'd ever spoken to — 17,000 in all. They wanted to hear what a I had to say. They filled the arena, and simulcast the event all over the base.

As I stood on stage in front of a sea of uniforms, I thought, how is this possible except through the grace of God? I had known nothing about military service just a decade before. I just wanted to write letters with a few of our troops overseas. Yet here I was, years later, sharing my story with 17,000 active duty service members.

Spreading the word about American Solider Network, and now our RuckUp program to help end veteran suicide, is one of the greatest joys of my life.

If you'd like me to speak at an event or meeting of your organization, please get in touch. I've included my booking information at the end of the book.

Same song, second verse

Shortly after I returned from my talk at MacDill, I was thrown another curve ball in the spring of 2018. I'd known for a few years that I had another tumor, but it was small and my medical team monitored it closely.

I had no symptoms for years, and suddenly I was getting severe headaches and throwing up. I called my surgeon.

We did a scan in July, and Dr. Giannotta came in to speak with me. In between catching up, as we have become dear friends over the past eight years, Dr. G (as I call him) in a very matter of fact tone said, "We've had great tumor management for years but this one has decided to start growing so we are going after it."

"I will meet with the team Monday and you'll get a call Tuesday to schedule your gamma knife surgery," he concluded.

With that he gave me a hug and was off to his next appointment.

I was numb and the lone drive back home in LA traffic from USC Keck Medical center was flooded with all sorts of thoughts, questions—and some fears.

The gamma knife surgery was *very* different than the craniotomy eight years prior. I checked in to Keck at 5:30 am for what was to be a six-hour visit. Yes—brain surgery as an "outpatient."

First, they put you under as they screw a metal head device (known as a halo) onto your skull. Once that is secure, they wake you up. No, it is not comfortable and as a matter of fact, it hurts! Then, a big clear plastic helmet looking shell is put on over the halo, followed by an MRI for "mapping" the tumor they are going to blast. That MRI was not like most. You're in the tube over 45 minutes and the loud, staccato, incessant banging of the machine is constant not intermittent.

The gamma knife procedure for me was about 40 minutes. The gamma knife machine is much like that of a large MRI except your head in the halo is screwed to the bed you lie on with your body strapped down to the bed as well. Everyone else leaves the room and they talk to you through an intercom from a remote location to you in the gamma knife.

It's a silent procedure so I asked for classic rock to serenade me. I figured I gotta keep it rockin' while this is happening, while my mind is, of course, thinking a million different thoughts.

Once the procedure is complete, you're rolled back into your room, the doctors come in to unscrew the device connected to your skull (you are awake for this ... ouch!) and after a little bit you are released home.

I still don't know exactly what kind of tumor it was the second time around, and at a certain point it doesn't matter. All that matters is that it wasn't cancer, and I survived... again. And that, after all, is my definition of resilience.

PILLAR #5

Develop your faith.

*" Have I not commanded you?
Be strong and courageous.
Do not be afraid; do not be
discouraged, for the Lord your
God will be with you
wherever you go."*

Joshua 1:9

Pillar #5: Develop your faith.

There's no other way to say this. To triumph over any adversity, you must have some sort of higher power. You've got to have faith.

Saturate your life in the power of positive of thinking. Start your day counting your blessings not your battles. Remind yourself of all the good in your life. Pour energy into feeding your mind with inspirational readings, music, books, audio books, lectures, anything that inspires and keeps you motivated. Develop a true prayer life and believe in the power of prayer.

The power of prayer

I've always had a church life. My parents were regular church goers, and although I wouldn't call them "Bible thumpers," God was always a part of our lives.

Faith is easy as a kid. Religion is Sunday mornings with Jesus stories. Faith is more challenging as an adult. When you're facing a crisis in your life, you're forced to dig deep and find that faith—or feel abandoned. Applying faith, really *working your faith* as an adult, that's the challenge.

I like to think of faith as a relationship, not a religion. Faith is letting yourself trust and let go. By letting go, I don't mean sitting by and doing nothing. You have to keep taking action, with faith that you're being guided and taken where you need to be.

When I had my first brain tumor, my dad was already gone and I really didn't want to burden my mom with it. I turned to scripture and devotional books to bolster my faith and keep it strong. And I prayed ... a lot!

For me, prayer isn't just asking for things to be alright or "please get me through this!" Prayer is a time to be grateful, to show true appreciation for what is. To ask for guidance and wisdom. Sometimes prayers are answered—and you know whatever it is came from God.

And, sometimes, prayers aren't answered they way we'd like them to be. (Or my dad would be still be here, right?)

There's a line in a Garth Brooks song about the greatest gifts being unanswered prayers. I figure if I'm still here, and I'm still breathing, then I still have work to do. That helps me find the courage I need.

Simple rituals

Faith can be a habit, and one with more rewards than you might think. Here are some simple ways that I incorporate everything I've talked about in this chapter in my daily life:

- Wake up and say prayers of thanksgiving. When something good happens, acknowledge it and be grateful to God!
- When things get tough (and they will), I find a quiet place to reset with a prayer of strength and compassion.
- Say a prayer every night before bed.
- Have scriptures sent to my phone. I use two apps: Bible for Women and d365dailydevotional.

- Post spiritual and faith-based stories and quotes on social media so that people who follow me will get an uplifting moment.
- While driving, I listen to faith-based music stations. It helps me to be in a state of grace and centeredness, whether I'm stuck in traffic or on a road trip through the desert.
- Every Sunday I try to get to a church service, but if I can't, I'll watch a Sunday service on YouTube. Both of the churches I belong to have a channel!

I keep the people I love and care about in my prayers. I pray for our military and for our leaders. And I pray for the President.

I met Mr. Trump on several occasions before he was elected and was privileged to be acquainted with him. Once he was elected, I sent him a letter of congratulations, encouragement and prayer for his administration, his family, and for his guidance while serving as President. I also committed to keeping him in prayer throughout his presidential service.

Never in a million years did I expect any reply, but I did receive a reply! I'm including a copy of it here. (Face it, no matter what party you support, it's kind of cool to get a letter on White House stationery!)

THE WHITE HOUSE
WASHINGTON

Dear Ann:

Thank you for your kind message and prayers.

The unwavering faith of the American people has sustained our country through the best and worst of times. As we look ahead, as one Nation, we will fulfill our sacred duty and deliver upon the promise of America for all of our people. We will strengthen our national spirit and ensure that America continues to shine as a beacon of freedom for all the world to see.

Melania and I are heartened by your support. Thank you for taking the time to share your thoughts and for keeping us in your prayers.

God Bless America,

[signature: Donald Trump]

WWW.WHITEHOUSE.GOV

Survive & thrive

I listen to a lot of Christian music; it especially helps to pass the time when I drive from my home in California to my mom's in Phoenix.

One day I heard this song by Zach Williams and knew I had to look up the lyrics and share them:

Survivor

For so long I carried the weight of my past
Cripple by burdens like stones on my back
I thought I had fallen too far from your grace
But you came and showed me the way

When I was lost soul searching
You were the ground beneath my feet
When I was blind man begging
You were the eyes so I could see
When the smoke was rising up
You were the air that I could breath
You gave me hope you gave me something to believe

Now I'm alive and born again
Rescued from the grip of sin
God your love came crashing in
And pulled me out of the fire
I'm a survivor

Now all I can see are the fields of your grace
Wherever I run your leading the way
You shook the shackles off my feet
I found redemption on my knees

You gave me hope you gave me something to believe

©2018 by Zach Williams; many thanks for his gracious approval to reprint. www.ZachWilliamsMusic.com

To me, these lyrics really speak to finding the strength and courage that you need to not only get through a crisis, but to come out the other side with more faith, more strength, and more resilience.

This is a fitting place to end this book. I'll close with a passage from one of my favorite books, *The Butterfly Effect* by Andy Andrews:

The very beating of your heart has meaning and purpose. Your actions have value far greater than silver or gold. Your life and what you do with it today matters forever.

Resources

American Soldier Network
www.americansoldiernetwork.org
RuckUp.org

Veterans Crisis Line
Dial 1-800-273-8255 and Press 1 to talk to someone.
-or-
Send a text message to **838255** to connect with a VA responder.

National Suicide Prevention Lifeline
1-800-273-8255

Additional Suicide Resources
www.cdc.gov/violenceprevention/suicide

Disaster Distress Helpline
www.samhsa.gov/find-help/disaster-distress-helpline

Healthy Brains
healthybrains.org/pillars/

US Veterans Magazine
www.usveteransmagazine.com

Impact Church
www.impactchurch.com

Crossline Church
www.crosslinechurch.com

American Psychological Association
www.apa.org/helpcenter/disaster

Recommended Reading

The Path: Creating Your Mission Statement for Work and for Life
By Laurie Beth Jones

His Needs Her Needs
By Willard F Harley Jr

The Will of God as a Way of Life
By Gerald L Sittser

In the Grip of Grace
By Max Lucado

JESUS CEO Using Ancient Wisdom for Visionary Leadership
By Laurie Beth Jones

Game Changer
By Travis Hearn

About the Author

For the past 15 years, Annie has dedicated her life to raising awareness for U.S. veterans of all eras. Annie successfully combatted post-traumatic stress herself in 1995 after being beaten by passengers while in flight working as a flight attendant. That same assault resulted in a fractured back that Annie still seeks treatment for today, some 20 years later. She subsequently survived six separate concussions and a life-threatening brain tumor in 2010. She awoke from a 10-hour surgery deaf in one ear and half of her face caved in and fallen. A two-year recovery journey followed where she learned to walk, talk, and cope with her new reality. A second brain tumor in 2018 failed to stop Annie's mission.

Annie relates to and inspires our heroes and others by her real-life battles. Annie has walked the walk and her inspirational talks ignite a flame of hope within all she comes in contact with.

She is the founder of The American Soldier Network, a 501(c)(3) charity based in southern California with marketing efforts extending across the USA. Annie's passion and compassion have drawn movie and TV stars, political figures and sports celebrities to join her crusade. Thanks to Annie, they offer their time, talents and energy here at home for our heroes.

Annie is creator of the TV series "American Heroes" and a columnist for *US Veterans Magazine* column "American Heroes" in every issue. In 2018 through her American Soldier Network, Annie created and launched RuckUp.org to be an indispensable and lifesaving resource for veterans, military and their families. Her "I Choose to Live" oath has been the first step in saving the lives of our heroes.

She has received numerous awards, citations and commendations, including the Open Heart Patriot Award (2012) from the Open Hearts Foundation; the Above and Beyond Award for Excellence (2016) from the Angel Light Academy; and the Helping Hands Award (2017) from the Celestial Awards of Excellence.

A Minnesota native who grew up in Southern California, Annie received a Theatre Arts scholarship at California State University Long Beach and studied at the American Film Institute. She found a niche in sports broadcasting and special events. She lives in Orange County with her Rhodesian Ridgeback dogs Hazel and Tex, and frequently visits her dear mom in Phoenix, Arizona.

Connect with Annie

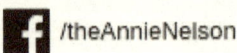 /theAnnieNelson   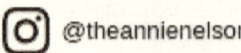 @theannienelson   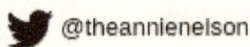 @theannienelson

Invite Annie to Speak

"Our group had Annie Nelson speak at our monthly meeting. She was awesome! She was very interesting and knowledgeable about the plight of our veterans. Some of her stories were heart-wrenching and brought a tear to your eyes with many of us. She really cares about our veterans and is doing something about it."
— Mary Kafka, VP-Programs, San Diego County Federation of Republican Women

Let Annie help you deliver great content that will have attendees ready to take action. She will generate impactful buzz with a talk that is completely customized for you and your audience. She will have audiences captivated with the story of her journey from being attacked on the job, causing lifelong injuries she has overcome, to surviving two brain tumor surgeries and six concussions and making advocating for veterans and active duty military her life's work. She founded the American Soldier Network, a nonprofit supporting our veterans and military helping thousands since its inception will keep audiences captivated. To inquire about Annie's availability, please email bookings@theannienelson.com.

www.ingramcontent.com/pod-product-compliance
Lightning Source LLC
Chambersburg PA
CBHW021952290426
44108CB00012B/1042